BUGS TO BUNNIES

Hands-On Animal Science Activities for Young Children

Kenn Goin

Eleanor Ripp

Kathleen Nastasi Solomon

illustrated by
Rochelle Valdivia

Chatterbox Press
New York
1989

For Joey, Kara, Kelly, and Kyle

Primary author of *Introduction*, *Reptiles*, and *Birds* is Kenn Goin.
Primary author of *All About Animals*, *Amphibians*, and *Mammals* is Eleanor Ripp.
Primary author of *Insects*, *Spiders*, and *Fish* is Kathleen Nastasi Solomon.

Address inquiries to: Chatterbox Press
                       PO Box 7933
                       FDR Station
                       New York, NY 10150-2411

Cover and text design: Elizabeth Alexander
Cover illustration: Susan T. Hall
Typesetting: Central Carolina Publishing
              Chapel Hill, NC

First published in the United States of America in 1989 by Chatterbox Press.

ISBN: 0-943129-03-6

10 9 8 7 6 5 4 3 2

Table of Contents

Introduction

*"As we feel for ourselves, we must feel for all forms of life—
the whales, the seals, the forests, the seas."*

from The Greenpeace Philosophy

When we're small, animals seem wonderful and mysterious. Some of them, we're sure, would make the best friends we could ever have. Others are a little strange and don't seem too friendly, but their very strangeness keeps our interest in them alive.

Our curiosity about animals increases as we listen to what our teachers and parents have to tell us. They read stories to us about lazy and hard-working insects ("The Grasshopper and the Ant"), and about slow reptiles and fast mammals ("The Tortoise and the Hare"). These stories introduce us to some of the values we'll need in life. Many of the stories awaken our imagination, such as the one about the handsome prince who was turned into the frog ("The Frog Prince"). After all, how could a person become an amphibian? Other stories, like the one about Miss Muffet and the Spider, puzzle us. They make us ask lots of questions. ("What are curds and whey?") Some stories that nearly break our hearts, like the one about the poor little bird in "The Ugly Duckling," make us start to realize that others have feelings and that it's important to treat everyone kindly.

Yes, we hear tales that involve every kind of animal—from scheming bugs to talking bunnies. The stories help us learn about our own feelings and about the world and the animals in it. They help us understand that animals are living things. It's no surprise that we want to know more about these fascinating creatures who share our world.

The Science of Animals

Bugs to Bunnies was created to help teachers and parents introduce young children to the *study* of animals. The activities in the book are designed to help youngsters learn about the real lives of animals in a gentle, appropriate manner.

All of the activities—such as building giant bird nests and making silver-bellied fish—are designed to provide simple, tangible ways of helping children grasp concepts that are most easily understood through hands-on experiences.

Science Goals

Good science begins with natural curiosity, and young children have an abundance of curiosity about animals. Our goal in *Bugs to Bunnies* has been to provide ways to answer the questions children most often ask about the creatures who share our planet: "What do they look like? Where do they live? What do they eat? How do they have babies? How do they defend themselves?"

If children learn specific facts about animals as a result of the stories and activities in this book, that's wonderful! But learning facts should not be the focus of science activities for young children. Rather, we want the children whose teachers and parents use this book to come to understand that there are many kinds of animals in the world. Some of them are very different from each other. Some are very similar. As living things, however, all of them need food, a place to live, a way to stay safe, and a way to have babies.

We also want children to ask lots of questions about animals, for good questions are the beginnings of good science. Use questions from the box on this page in class, and children will soon learn to ask these questions themselves.

As you work with children, help them
- learn to watch animals carefully. ["How do they move?" "What color are they?" "What sounds do they make?"]
- learn to ask questions about things that make them curious. ["Why is that bird so green?"]
- learn to make guesses about the reasons things seem to be a certain way. ["That bird is probably green so it can hide among the leaves of the trees."]
- learn that it is important for scientists to keep records of what they see. ["I'd better draw a picture of that green bird I saw today!"]

These simple steps will help prepare them for the science they will encounter in the future.

ANIMAL QUESTIONS

1. What do we call an animal that looks like this?
2. How does it move?
3. How does it see?
4. How many eyes does it have?
5. What color are its eyes?
6. Does it have eyelashes?
7. How does it hear?
8. Where are its ears?
9. What color and shape are its ears?
10. How does it eat?
11. What does it eat?
12. How does it breathe? How can you tell?
13. Does it sleep? How can you tell?
14. When does it sleep?
15. How do we take care of its home?

OPEN-ENDED QUESTIONS

1. What would happen if...?
2. How can we find out ...?
3. How could you be sure that ...?
4. How can we do ...?
5. How many ways can we ...?
6. Where could we find ...?
7. What happened to ...?
8. What do you think ...?

The Eight Units

Bugs to Bunnies is divided into eight units. The first unit is called All About Animals. It will help you teach your very youngest children the differences between *living* and *non-living things*, and between *animals* and *plants*. Each of the other seven units in the book covers a particular animal group:

- Insects
- Reptiles
- Birds
- Spiders
- Fish
- Mammals
- Amphibians

Within the Units

Each unit covers five aspects of an animal group:
1) *characteristics* or "What does the animal look like?"
2) *diet* or "What does the animal eat?"
3) *defenses* or "How does the animal protect itself?"
4) *habitat* or "Where does the animal live?"
5) *reproduction* or "How does the animal have babies?"

There is also a sixth section in each unit (except in All About Animals) that introduces a special animal. These sections have been included so that you can help children study a specific member of each group *in-depth*.

- insects—butterflies
- fish—sharks
- spiders—tarantulas
- birds—penguins
- amphibians—frogs
- mammals—rabbits
- reptiles—crocodiles

Each section within a unit—characteristics, diet, etc.—includes a *story* to introduce the concepts, a page of *activity* ideas for large and small groups, and one or more *science sheets* that can be reproduced and given to children to help reinforce what has been learned in the stories and activities. [See page 6.]

Where to Begin?

The units in *Bugs to Bunnies* are self-contained. You may teach them in any order that you choose. Once you've selected a unit, however, it's best to begin your presentation with the first story and proceed from there. By the time you've read aloud each of the stories in the unit and followed them up with as many of the activities and science sheets as you feel are appropriate, the children will have a good understanding of the animal group you've been focusing on. Always feel free to adjust activities to meet the needs of your students and the realities of your classroom.

Resources

We've included addresses of places to write or call for certain materials within each unit. Some of the most useful sources for science materials are:

Carolina Biological Supply
2700 York Road
Burlington, NC 27215-3398
1-800-334-5551

Delta Education, Inc.
PO Box M
Nashua, NH 03061
1-800-258-1302

Insect Lore Products
PO Box 1535
Shafter, CA 93263
1-805-746-6047

You'll also find a list of books on page 186 that are appropriate to use in teaching various kinds of animals. Some of these books are storybooks, some are books with wonderful animal pictures, and some are science books. The more resources you can bring into your classroom, the better.

Real, Live Animals!

Of course, nothing is better for a hands-on approach to animal science than live animals. You'll find ideas in each unit for bringing animals into the classroom and for getting children in touch with animals outside the classroom.

Even though we hope that you'll try to bring at least one specimen of each kind of animal that you study into class, you'll find hundreds of activities in this book that will help children learn about animals even when live specimens are not available.

Kinds of Pages in *Bugs to Bunnies*

Objective: To learn that birds have no teeth and that birds eat different kinds of food—primarily fruits and/or seeds, insects, fish, or small animals.

Dinner with My Bird Friends

One day I invited all of my bird friends for dinner. Having birds over for dinner can be tricky because birds have no teeth. You have to have exactly the kind of food they are used to eating—or they'll go hungry. Here's a list of the birds I invited to my dinner party.

The sparrow, who sometimes lives in the forest and sometimes in the city, loves to eat all kinds of seeds. So I had sunflower, corn, and sesame seeds for him.

The toucan, who looks a lot like a parrot with his brightly colored feathers, lives in the jungle. His favorite meal is fresh fruit—papayas and mangoes and bananas. Yum, yum, yum!

The woodpecker likes to eat little bugs. Where do you think Woodpecker lives? (in a hollow tree in the forest) ■ I served Woodpecker a dish of earthworms and spiders!

Mother Pelican loves the taste of fish. She lives close to the water because she hardly ever eats anything that doesn't come from the sea. I gave her some tuna. What would you have fed Pelican?

■ The hawk and owl are hunters. They like to eat rats and snakes and sometimes other birds! Most of their neighbors are pretty careful around them. I asked these two to bring their own food!

If you had bird friends over for dinner, which birds would you invite? ■ What would you feed them?

138

Stories

In each unit, there are stories about the animal's physical *characteristics*, its *diet*, *defenses*, *habitat*, and *reproduction*. All stories are simple, age-appropriate tales designed to appeal to young children. The black boxes ■ in the story text will help you refind your place in reading if you stop for discussion after one of the questions in the text.

❑ **Feeding Time**

1 Field trips. Plan a field trip to a zoo or pet store with the children. Call ahead so that you can arrive at a time when the birds are being fed.

2 Bird feeders. Feeders are a good way to attract birds for youngsters to observe. Before you build one of the feeders described on this page, buy one of the inexpensive bird guides listed under *Resources* and, if your budget allows, a pair of inexpensive binoculars. These items will make watching the birds that dine at your feeder a truly entertaining and educational experience.

❑ **Pinecone Feeder**

You need: string, pinecone, knife, peanut butter

Tie a string around the base of the pinecone. Use a knife to press peanut butter all over the cone. [Explain to children that peanut butter is seeds, and birds that like seeds will eat the peanut butter.] Hang the cone from a tree limb and watch!

❑ **Milk Carton Feeder**

You need: hole puncher or knife; empty, clean milk carton; string or yarn; bird seed

Punch a hole in the top of the empty carton (as shown), and thread string or yarn through it. Cut out the center portion of each side panel, leaving about a 1" frame all around. Put bird seed in the bottom of the carton. Hang your feeder outside.

What Do Birds Eat?	
fruits / seeds	insects / spiders / worms

❑ **Bird Food Bulletin Board**

You need: yarn
light-colored construction paper
marker
magazines and scissors
tacks
(optional) bird seed and tweezers

1 Preparing the board. Use yarn to divide a bulletin board into two sections. On each of three strips of construction paper, use a marker to write one of the following: fruits/seeds, insects/spiders/worms, and What Do Birds Eat? Place the strips on the board as shown.

2 Filling the board. Find at least one picture of each of the birds described below (or enlarge the pictures on page 138 and cut them out). Post each picture in the appropriate section of the board.

❑ *insect specialist* (woodpecker, cuckoo, flycatcher, etc.)—prefers insects, spiders, or worms, but may also eat seeds, nuts, etc.

❑ *fruit and seed lover* (sparrow, dove, pigeon, etc.)—prefers fruits and/or seeds, but may also eat insects, spiders, and worms

3 Involving the class. Explain that each kind of bird has a body that helps it find and eat the special kinds of food it needs. Birds that eat seeds and insects need bills that make it easy to pick up tiny things. Often these birds have short bills that work like tweezers. [Let children try to pick up small seeds with tweezers.]

Explain that seed eaters can often spend the winter in very cold areas while insect eaters cannot. Why? [Because insects disappear in very cold weather while seeds remain abundant.]

Have children cut pictures of foods from various magazines and books and paste them in the appropriate sections of the bulletin board.

Extension idea! Create a similar bulletin board using birds of prey (hawks, owls, vultures, etc.) and birds who eat seafood (pelicans, flamingos, cranes, etc.).

Resources: Bird Guides

❑ Golden Bird Guides
❑ Peterson Bird Guides

Science Sheet Notes

Birds That Hunt, page 140—Use this page to introduce your students to birds of prey. Teach children the major birds-of-prey groups: vultures, hawks, and falcons. Children will be interested to learn that all of these birds hunt during the day. Some eat relatively large animals (rattlesnakes, rabbits, etc.). Many of the birds are very large. The California condor, for example, has a wingspan of 10 feet. [The California condor, unfortunately, is almost extinct.]

We Love Vegetables!, page 141—The majority of birds eat a combination of seeds and insects. The birds on this page, however, prefer a diet of plant foods. This sheet presents an excellent opportunity to study one of America's favorite birds in depth—the turkey. Turkeys are good runners. They eat acorns, fruits, and seeds. Only the male turkey (Tom, by name) gobbles. He gobbles to call his sweethearts home to the harem!

139

Large and Small Group Activities

The activities that follow each story include experiments, crafts, language and counting activities, and motor games related to the information in the story.

Name _____

Birds That Hunt

Color the birds. Cut out the pictures. Paste each picture onto its matching outline.
[See page 139.]

eagle   owl   hawk   falcon

140

Science Sheets

These pages will help you reinforce the material covered in the stories and activities.

All About Animals

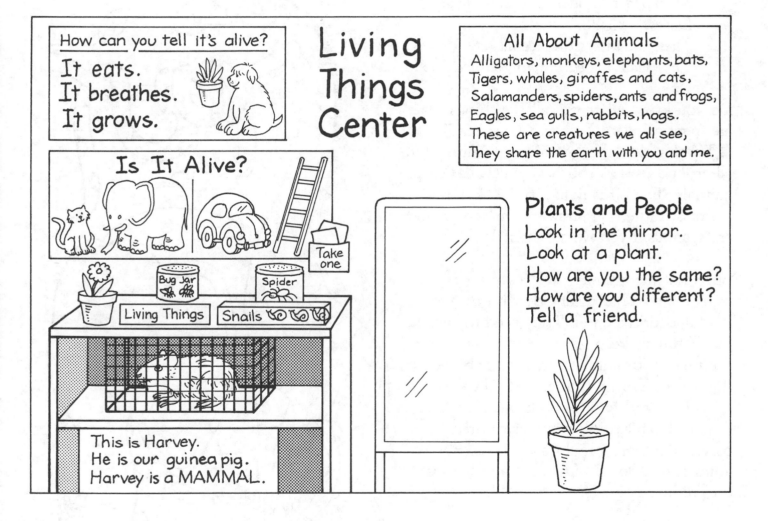

How can you tell it's alive?

It eats.
It breathes.
It grows.

Living Things Center

All About Animals
Alligators, monkeys, elephants, bats,
Tigers, whales, giraffes and cats,
Salamanders, spiders, ants and frogs,
Eagles, sea gulls, rabbits, hogs.
These are creatures we all see,
They share the earth with you and me.

Is It Alive?

Take one

Bug Jar

Spider

Living Things

Snails

This is Harvey.
He is our guinea pig.
Harvey is a MAMMAL.

Plants and People
Look in the mirror.
Look at a plant.
How are you the same?
How are you different?
Tell a friend.

Objective: To learn that animals are living things. They eat, drink, breathe, move, grow, and have babies.

All About Animals

Alligators, monkeys, elephants, bats,
Tigers, whales, giraffes, and cats,
Salamanders, spiders, ants, and frogs,
Eagles, sea gulls, rabbits, hogs.
These are things that we all see,
They share the earth with you and me.

Do you know what we call the things that are mentioned in the poem I just read? ■ That's right—they're animals. Animals are all around us. Do you have a pet? ■ Pets are animals. The birds flying in the sky are animals. Little bugs crawling on the ground are animals. Even we are animals.

But what are animals? ■ We say they are *living things*. That means they have to eat food and drink water. They need to breathe too. Animals keep growing and changing all the time, and animals can have babies of their own. Things that are not alive can't do any of these things. A rock can't eat food. A pencil can't drink water or breathe. A bicycle can't grow and have babies. But animals can do all of these things because they're living things.

Animals come in many sizes—some are very big, like elephants. Others are tiny, like ants. Animals have different shapes—some are tall and skinny like giraffes, and others are round and plump like hippopotamuses. Still others are long and slinky like snakes!

And animals live in different places. They live in wet places, dry places, icy cold places, and hot places. They live in high places, low places, and even in the water. In fact, animals live almost everywhere. When you go out to play today, look around for animals. How many do you think you'll see?

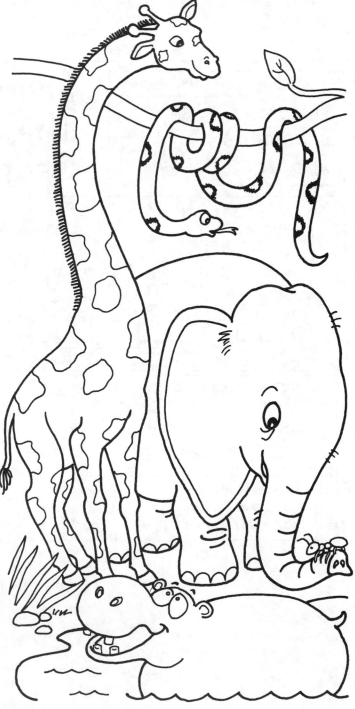

8

Animals

frog

turtle

owl

lion

dog

fish

spider

butterfly

❑ Living and Non-Living Collages

1 First review the characteristics of living things. Write them on a chart, and display the chart in the living things center.

> **Living Things**
> They need food.
> They need water.
> They need to breathe.
> They grow and change.
> They can have babies.

2 Then label one large sheet of construction paper *Living Things* and another sheet *Non-Living Things*. Have children bring in magazine pictures of living and non-living things.
3 In class, let children sort the pictures and paste them onto the correct sheet to create the two collages. Display at the living things center.

❑ Living Things Center

1 Explain that there is another kind of living thing besides animals. These living things are called plants. You can tell the difference between plants and animals because animals move around from place to place, while plants stay in one place. That's because plants are attached to the soil they are planted in. Plants *make* their own food from the soil and the air. Animals must *find* their food.
2 At your living things center, place a variety of plants in one section and different animals (lizards, frogs, insects) in a second section.

❑ "Animals and Plants" Poem

To reinforce the difference between animals and plants, teach the poem below. Have children illustrate it. Then write the poem on oaktag and display it with the drawings.

Animals are living things,
They move from place to place,
They have to find the foods they eat,
And it's a lifelong chase.

Plants are also living things,
Their roots are in the soil,
*The food they eat they make themselves,**
They cannot move at all.

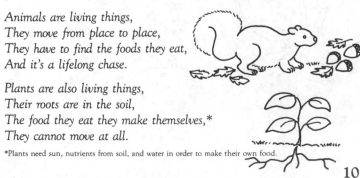

*Plants need sun, nutrients from soil, and water in order to make their own food.

❑ "Is It Alive?" Game

Here's a game to help children learn to distinguish between living things (animals and plants) and non-living things.

You need: crayons or markers
copy of page 13 and page 14
glue
4-5 large oaktag sheets
scissors
large envelope

1 Color the pictures on pages 13 and 14, and mount the pages on oaktag.
2 Cut out the pictures. [If you wish, laminate the pictures for extra durability.]
3 At the top of one oaktag sheet, draw a small picture of a dog next to a tree to represent living things. At the top of the other sheet, draw a rock next to a hammer to represent non-living things. For older children, label the tops of the sheets *Living* and *Non-Living*.
4 Put the pictures in a large envelope and place them along with the oaktag sheets in the science center. Lay the sheets on a flat surface. Ask children to take the pictures out of the envelope and place each one on the correct sheet. [Two children can sort by taking turns at placing the pictures.]

❑ "How Animals Move" Bulletin Board

You need: 5 different colors of construction paper, one
lighter than the others
large manila envelope
dark marker
mounted animal pictures

1 Back a bulletin board with light-colored construction paper. Place four different-colored sheets across the board as shown below. Use a dark marker to write the title *How Animals Move* and the labels *Walk*, *Swim*, *Crawl*, and *Fly*.
2 Add an envelope near the bottom of the bulletin board and write the words "Take One" on it.
3 Place pictures of a wide variety of animals in the envelope. [You can use pictures from pages 22, 57, 83, 122, 148-149, and 161 of this book, or have children draw pictures of animals they love. You can even use animal stencils.]
4 Let individual children take pictures from the envelope and use tape to place them in the correct category on the bulletin board.

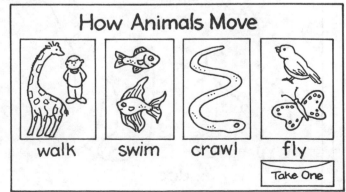

❑ "Sounds of Nature" Game

You need: 10-15 pictures of animals mounted on oaktag
big box

1 To play this game, place pictures of different animals in a big box.

2 Without looking in the box, each child, in turn, takes a picture from the box and imitates the sound that the animal makes. [If children are too young or too reticent, have children pick a card and hand it to you for you to make the sound.]

3 The rest of the class must guess the name of the animal.

4 After all the guesses have been made, the child shows the class the picture. Some animals to include are a dog, cat, horse, cow, rooster, pig, turkey, lion, frog, and bee.

❑ *Sylvester and the Magic Pebble*

Read aloud *Sylvester and the Magic Pebble* by William Steig. This heart-warming story tells about a donkey that becomes a pebble. Children will empathize with Sylvester's problems and start to develop an understanding of what it means to be a non-living thing. (pebble) Ask children: What can't Sylvester do when he is a pebble? [He can't move, eat, or grow. He can't do anything but remain in one place all the time.] Would you like to be a non-living thing? Why or why not? Which non-living thing would you be? Children can dictate their ideas to you and then illustrate their stories.

❑ Taping Animal Sounds

A fun-filled activity is to record animal sounds, and have children play a game to see who can name each animal first. As an alternative, record individual youngsters making animal sounds. Have the class try to guess the names of the animals being imitated.

❑ "Name That Animal" Game

You need: 9 animal cards (from pages 13-14)
large sheet of oaktag
black marker
penny
small marker for each player (paper clip, eraser, jack)

1 Reproduce only the nine animal cards from pages 13-14. [You do not need the other cards for this activity.]

2 Glue the animal cards onto the oaktag sheet to create a game board, as shown below.

3 Use the black marker to draw the arrows and to write the words *Start* and *Finish* as shown below.

4 Children place their markers on *Start*. Each player then takes turns tossing the penny. Players move ahead one space for heads and two spaces for tails.

5 Each player must name the animal he or she lands on. If the answer is incorrect, a player moves back one space at a time till he or she can name the animal.

6 The first player to reach *Finish* wins the game.

7 To extend the use of the game, change the animal pictures periodically.

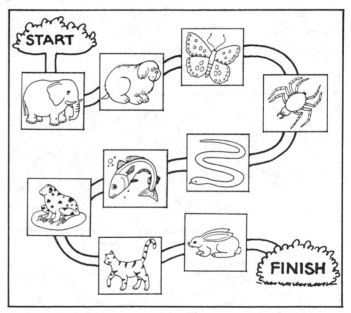

Science Sheet Notes

Is This an Animal?, page 12—Point out that all the pictures on this page show living things, but not all of the living things are animals. Review how animals are different from plants. [They can move from place to place, they need to find their own food.] Then have children complete the page.

Is It Alive?, pages 13-14—Use these cards with the "Is It Alive?" game on page 10 and with the "Name That Animal" game on this page.

Name _____

Is This an Animal?

Circle the animals. [See page 11.]

12

Is It Alive?

[See page 10.]

Is It Alive?

[See page 10.]

Insects

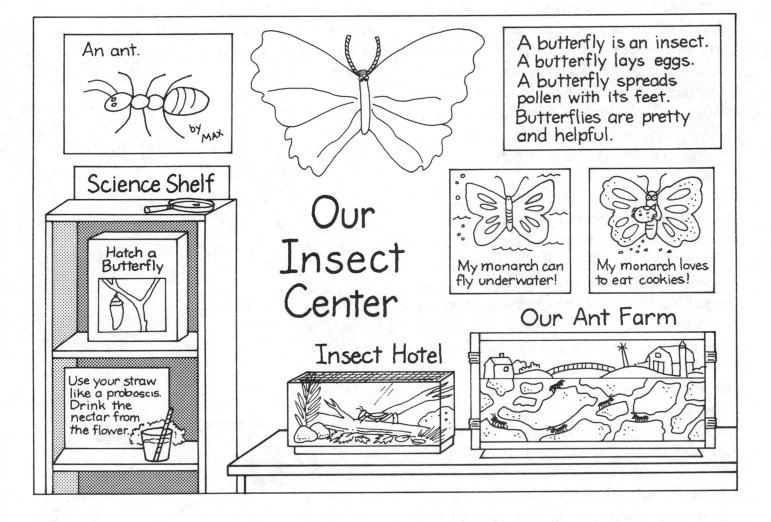

An ant.
by MAX

A butterfly is an insect.
A butterfly lays eggs.
A butterfly spreads
pollen with its feet.
Butterflies are pretty
and helpful.

Science Shelf

Hatch a
Butterfly

Use your straw
like a proboscis.
Drink the
nectar from
the flower.

Our
Insect
Center

Insect Hotel

My monarch can
fly underwater!

My monarch loves
to eat cookies!

Our Ant Farm

Objective: To learn the different body parts of insects and how they function.

What Is An Insect?

Some animals are very big and some are very small. But there is one type of animal that is often very, very small. In fact, this animal is sometimes so tiny that you hardly notice it—until it lands on your arm or bites your leg! Do you know this animal's name? ■ Yes, we call some of these animals bugs—water bugs, bedbugs, stink bugs. But scientists call these bugs insects!

All insects have six legs. Some insects have two wings and others have four wings. All insects have two feelers on top of their head. These feelers are also called antennae (an-ten-ī). An insect uses its antennae to feel things, to smell things, and sometimes even to hear things. Insects also have tiny hairs all over their bodies to help them feel. Insects are different than people because they have no bones inside their bodies. Instead, they have a tough skin on the outside to protect them, and underneath that skin is an even tougher shell that is like armor.

People breathe through two little holes in their nose called nostrils, but insects breathe through small tubes on the bottoms of their bellies! How do you think it would feel to breathe through your belly button? ■ Try it. Can you do it? ■ Of course not! Only insects can. Most insects have two large eyes,

but a few insects have even more than two. However, insects can't see very well at all.

There are nearly one million types of insects, and they are all different. Some, like fleas, are as tiny as freckles; and others, like walking sticks, are as long as your whole finger!

Big or small, fast or slow—all insects are part of nature's plan and can help people in many ways. Aren't we lucky to be able to share the earth with such interesting animals?

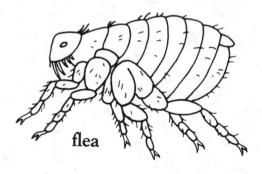
flea

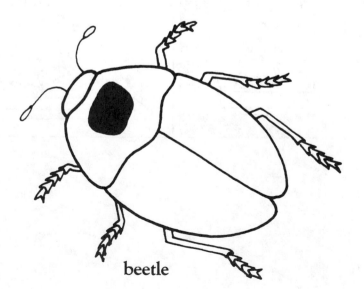
beetle

16

Anatomy of an Insect

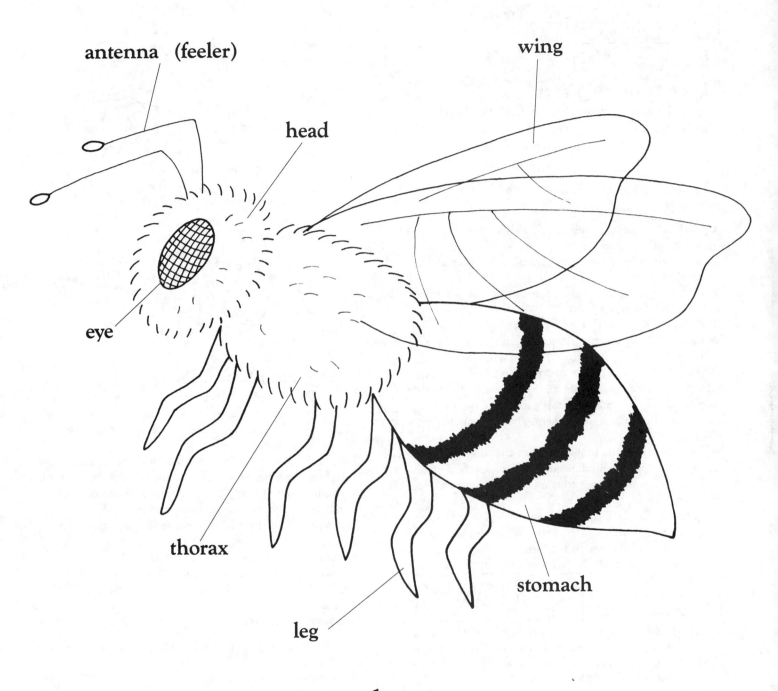

antenna (feeler)

wing

head

eye

thorax

leg

stomach

bee

Vocabulary

antennae—the threadlike sense organs (feelers) on the heads of insects and other animals

armor—any hard (shell-like) protective covering

☐ My Favorite Insect

It's fun and easy to record your student's favorite insects!

You need: scissors
5 colors of construction paper
5 small baskets or bowls
oaktag
markers or crayons
ruler and glue

1 Choose five popular insects. [Good choices include: ants, bees, mosquitoes, fireflies, grasshoppers, walking sticks, crickets, butterflies.] Find a picture of each insect chosen and paste it on a bowl.

2 Cut 3″ squares from each color of construction paper. Put a different color in each bowl.

3 Prepare a graph with the insects you've selected listed.

4 Read the story on page 16 to the class. Then discuss the different insects you've listed on the graph.

5 Ask children what their favorite insect is. Have each child choose a colored square that represents his or her favorite insect. Ask the children to draw pictures of their chosen insects on the squares, label them, and write their names on the squares.

6 Hold up the blank graph. Explain that a graph is a special way to show us information quickly. Have each child glue his or her construction paper square in the appropriate place on the graph.

7 After the graph is completed, ask: "Which insect has the most squares? Which has the least? Which insects have the same number of squares? Which insect is the most popular? Which is least popular? Which insect would you like to have as a pet?"

☐ Insect Hotel

1 The hotel. Make a vivarium using a covered aquarium tank. Put dirt and some leaves on the bottom of the tank. Add a few twigs, a small log, and some rocks. [A plant such as moss is a colorful addition.]

2 The guests. To get insects for the vivarium, sprinkle some crumbs or pour a few drops of honey in a place (inside or outside) where insects are likely to be found. Wait a couple of hours (or a few minutes) to see which insects come to eat. Capture one or two insects in a plastic container or small net and transfer them to your hotel. Put crumbs in with the insects.

You also may find insects on tree leaves or bushes. If you find an insect on a leaf, be sure to place the leaf in the vivarium with the insect.

3 Observation. Have children look at the insects through a magnifier. Help them note the following:
☐ 3 different body parts
☐ 2 antennae
☐ 2 or 4 eyes
☐ 6 legs
☐ 2 or more wings
☐ the way the insect moves

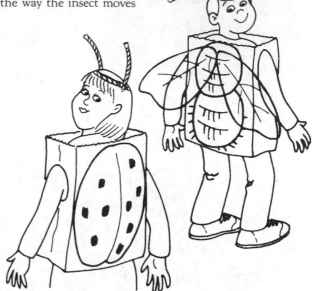

☐ Bug Bash Insect Party

1 Help children make insect costumes like the ones shown on this page. Use tin foil to make antennae crowns; make wings from oaktag; and use paper grocery bags to create insect body jackets.

2 Make *Walking Stick Treats* for the party by sticking small pretzel logs together with peanut butter. Make *Ants On a Log* by stuffing celery (or apple quarters) with cream cheese (or peanut butter) and covering with raisin ants. Make *Grasshopper Punch* by adding green food coloring to apple juice.

3 Make up bug stories with the children.

4 Play insect games. For example, change the words of "Duck, Duck, Goose" to fit a game called "Fly, Fly, Cricket."

Resources: Insects

Here's where to get catalogs that include giant ant farms and bug books and bottles.

☐ Insect Lore Products; PO Box 1535; Shafter, CA 93263; Phone 1-805-746-6047

☐ Delta Education, Inc.; PO Box M; Nashua, NH 03061; Phone 1-800-258-1302

☐ Carolina Biological Supply Co.; 2700 York Road; Burlington, NC 27215-3398; Phone 1-800-334-5551

Science Sheet Notes

Leg Count, page 19—Remind children that insects have six legs. Then give them this science sheet to complete.

Name _____

Leg Count

Insects have 6 legs. Count the legs on the bugs below. Circle the ones that are insects. Color them. [See page 18.]

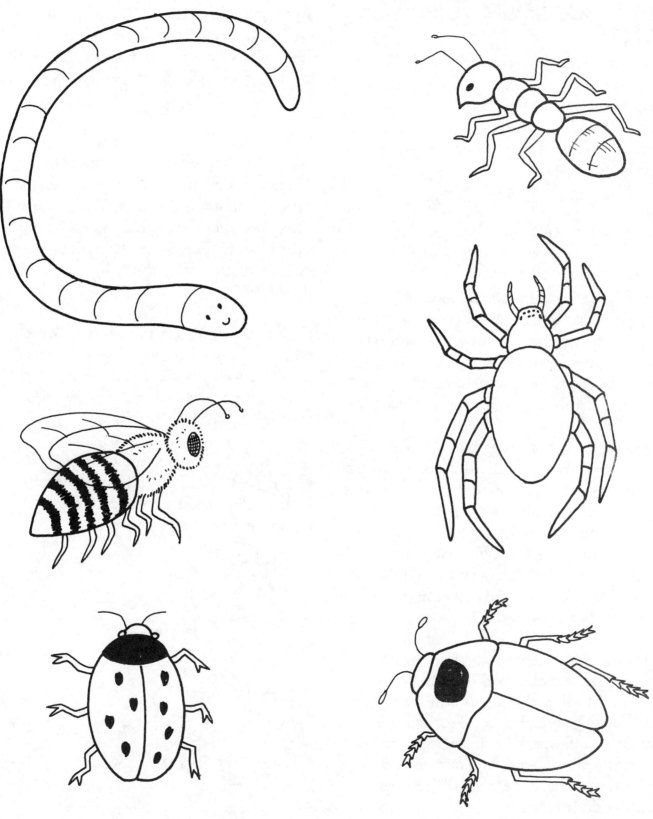

Objective: To learn that insects eat plants, other insects, and people's food.

Uninvited Guests

Have you ever gone on a picnic? ■ Then you know that as soon as you take out your food, insects come! Flies walk on your watermelon. Ants take away your bread crumbs. And bees buzz around to get a taste of your sweet peach!

Insects don't only eat people food. They also eat plants, and some insects even eat other insects. Caterpillars are hungry insects who love to munch on trees and leaves. When they grow up, they become butterflies, and then they drink the nectar inside flowers.

Dragonflies, on the other hand, are meat eaters—they love tasty mosquitoes. Ladybugs eat tiny insects called aphids. It's the praying mantis, however, who is the greatest insect hunter of all. It gobbles up lots and lots of flies and mosquitoes at one meal! That makes the praying mantis very helpful to people. Do you know why? (because it eats pesty insects that spread disease)

■ Another insect that sometimes helps people is the grasshopper. It munches on ants and fruitflies that can harm a farmer's crops. But the grasshopper also eats the corn growing in a farmer's field, and that makes the farmer very angry! The farmer doesn't want insects to eat the corn. Who does he want the corn eaten by?

■ Some insects eat old, rotten plants, garbage, and even dead insects. Termites live in rotten trees and old wood. If they get into a person's house, they can eat so much of the wood used to build the house that it will fall down! Cockroaches not only eat scraps from people's food, they also eat soap, hair, and glue. Yuk!   termite

Most insects eat the way people do—by tasting and chewing with their mouths. There are some insects, such as ants and bees, that also taste with their antennae. They touch food with the antennae to see if they'll like it! There are two insects—flies and moths—that actually taste their food with their feet!

Do you think insects have teeth? ■ If you said "No," then you were right! Insects do not have teeth. But crickets, beetles, and some other insects have sharp jaws for tearing and chewing food.

So now what do you think insects eat? ■ They eat just about anything! Insects are garbage disposals that eat people food, plants, and even other insects!

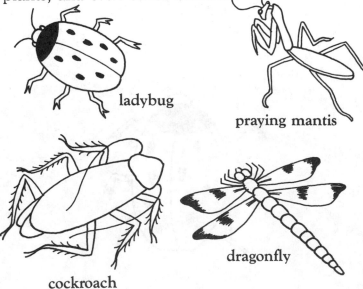

ladybug

praying mantis

cockroach

dragonfly

Vocabulary

mandible—the mouth parts of an insect that are used for biting

pollination—the transfer of yellow dust, called pollen, from one flower to another. Pollen is necessary for flowers to make seeds. Seeds are needed for new plants.

nectar—the sweet liquid that bees and other insects drink from inside a flower

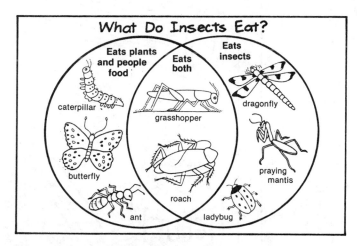

❏ **What Do Insects Eat? Bulletin Board**

A Venn Diagram is a very simple way to classify things that overlap. This is an activity for the whole class.

You need: insect pictures (from magazines or page 22)
black marker
butcher paper

1 Prepare the bulletin board as shown (hula-hoops are helpful in making the circles).

2 Read the story on page 20 to the children. Discuss insects that eat plants and people food (caterpillars, butterflies, ants); those that prefer to eat other insects (dragonflies, ladybugs, praying mantises); and those that eat both plants and insects (grasshoppers, cockroaches). Show the children the Venn Diagram and explain it.

3 Then give each child a picture of an insect. It's okay if several children have pictures of the same kind of insect. Ask each child which circle or category his or her picture belongs in. Then have the child (with lots of guidance) place the picture in the appropriate place on the diagram.

4 When group time is over, have a smaller group of children glue the pictures in place.

❏ **Jaws of Steel!**

You need: 1 nutcracker
small bowl filled with pieces of apple or with crackers

1 Explain that some insects, such as crickets and beetles, have very strong jaws called mandibles. They use their mandibles to crush and tear food.

2 Tell children that the nutcracker works like the cricket's two mandibles. Show the children how the nutcracker can crush the apple pieces or crackers. Let each child use the nutcracker. Place on a tray in your science center.

❏ **Picnic Pals — A Mural**

You need: 5′ sheet of butcher paper
tempera paints and brushes
stapler
1½′ piece of fabric
copies of page 22
crayons and scissors

1 Paint a horizontal line across the center of the butcher paper. Paint clouds, sun, and blue sky over the line and green grass below it.

2 Staple a piece of fabric to the paper to represent the picnic cloth. Draw some food and a person near the fabric if you wish.

3 Now give children copies of page 22 to color. Have them cut out, label, and place the insects near the food that insects might eat on the mural. Children can also draw, color, and cut out their own insects. (bees, flies, mosquitoes, wasps, ants, and caterpillars) Title your mural, *Picnic Pals*.

❏ **Insect Diet Checklist**

✔ Study how bees make honey.

✔ Watch an ant take its food home.

✔ Set up insect study groups. Have each group read about one insect's dietary habits and report back to the class. Nonreaders can read with older children or student teachers.

Science Sheet Notes

What Do I Eat?, page 22—Use this sheet after children have listened to the story on page 20. This sheet is also an excellent follow-up for the activities on this page.

Name _____

What Do I Eat?

Cut out the insect food pictures along the dotted lines. Paste each picture next to the insect it goes with. [See page 21.]

bee

termite

cockroach

caterpillar

dragonfly

GLUE

22

Objective: To learn that insects are protected from enemies by camouflage, by their ability to sting, and by their ability to escape.

Flee, Fight, or Hide?

Insects are among the smallest animals on earth, so they have many enemies. How do you think they protect themselves?

■ Some insects blend in with their surroundings so that other animals cannot see them. When animals can hide in this way, we say they are *camouflaged*. A grass-hopper is green, so where do you think it can hide and be camouflaged? (in the grass or on a green leaf) ■ Many moths are brown or gray so they often hide on the bark of trees. A praying mantis is large and green. It hides by standing very still among the green leaves of a plant. Most animals don't even see it till it moves to fly away. Can you guess how a walking stick hides from its enemies? ■ Because it looks like a twig, it can hide on a branch or tree limb!

Now there are other insects that will fight animals that are dangerous to them. How do bees and wasps keep enemies away? ■ They sting! Ants and tiger beetles have strong jaws. When they bite, it really hurts. Can you guess what the skunk beetle can do? ■ Yes, it sprays enemies with a chemical that stinks!

When there is danger nearby, many insects try to escape. Dragonflies have large powerful wings that help them fly away. Can you guess how crickets and grasshoppers get away from their enemies? ■ That's right—they hop away on their strong legs! Have you ever tried to catch a cricket?

■ An insect is a very small animal with many enemies. Birds, bats, and lizards eat insects. Even insects eat insects. People are always trying to get rid of pesty insects with poison sprays that kill them. As you can see, insects have lots of reasons to worry. How would you defend yourself if you were an insect?

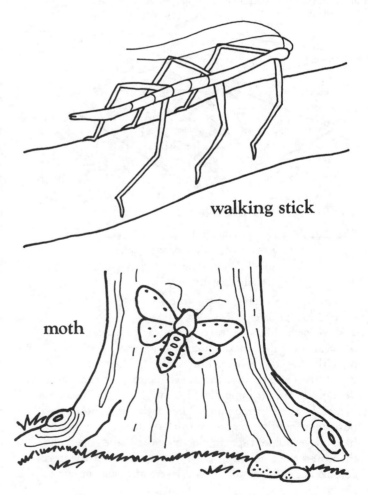

walking stick

moth

Vocabulary

camouflage—When an animal's body covering (feathers, hair, scales, etc.) is similar in color to the surroundings that the animal lives in, we say that one of the animal's natural defenses is camouflage.

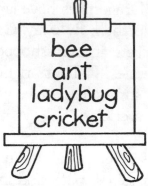

❑ Insect Brainstorming!

Ask children to name every kind of insect they can think of. This is a good way to find out how many insects children know. The activity also provides an opportunity to help children learn that all "bugs" are not insects; when someone names "spiders" as an insect, you can remind him or her that spiders have two more legs than insects. List the insects that are named on experience chart paper and display.

❑ Tissue Camouflage

You need: insect pictures from pages 19, 22, or 25
white construction paper
colored tissue paper
glue diluted with water

1 Make enough copies of the insect pictures for each child to have one picture.
2 Give each child one insect cutout and a piece of white construction paper. Have children color the cutouts and then paste them to the construction paper.
3 Tell the children that the insects need to be camouflaged. Remind them that camouflaged means "that the insects are hidden by their surroundings." Let each child choose a color of tissue paper that he or she thinks will help the insect hide. Have children spread glue over the tissue paper, and then press the gluey side of the tissue paper over the insect cutout. Let children add several layers of tissue paper if they like.
4 Display finished pieces in your room.

❑ Insects and Hunter

This is a good activity for groups of four or five children.
1 Choose some lively music and have it ready to play before you begin this activity.
2 Appoint one child to be the hunter. Ask each of the other children to choose an insect to pantomime. Have children name the insects they've chosen. Then ask the children how their insects defend themselves against enemies: do they fly away, hop away, hide, sting? Tell children that when you put on music, the hunter will come for them. They must use their insects' defenses to keep from being touched by the hunter. Tagged insects must sit down. Each time the music stops, the hunter and insects must freeze in place.
3 Start and stop the music as long as there's interest in the activity. Give everyone an opportunity to be hunter and insect.

❑ Insect Defenses Checklist

✔ Have children use modeling clay or dough to create imaginary insects. Have them give each insect a name and tell how it defends itself.
✔ Help children capture a fly. How does it try to get away? Repeat the activity with other insects (an ant, a moth, etc.).
✔ Ask children to look around the school yard or the classroom for places that insects use to hide. Make a list of their findings.

Science Sheet Notes

Insect Matching, page 25—Make a copy of this page and then cut along the dotted lines to remove the riddles from the game board. Next, make a copy of the game board for each child. Pass out the game boards and beans (or other tokens) to the children. Read each riddle and ask children to call out the answer and then place a bean (or other token) on the matching picture.

Give older children the riddles and the board. Ask them to cut apart the riddles and paste each riddle under the picture it goes with. Have them color the pictures.

Insect Matching

[See instructions on page 24.]

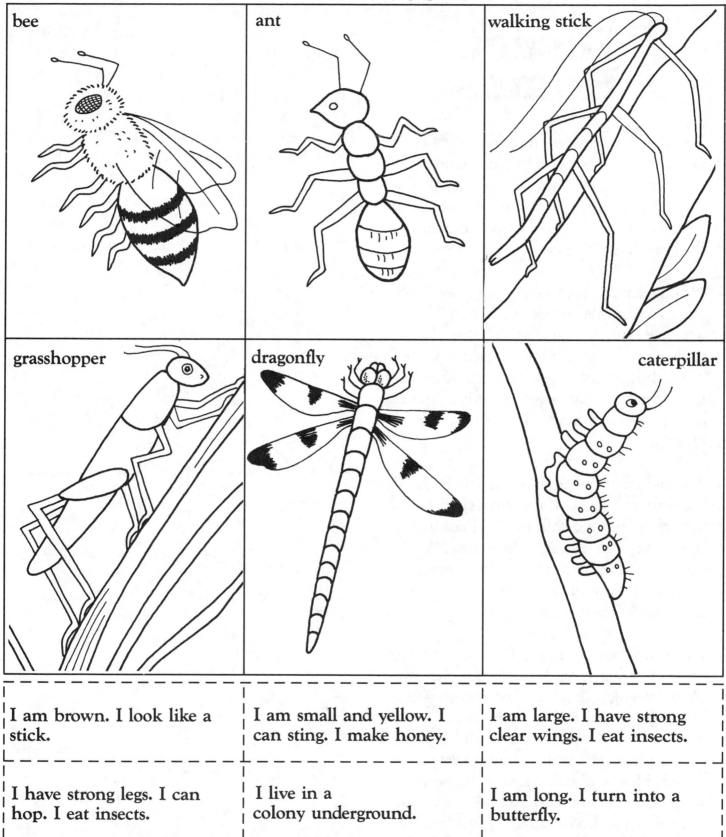

bee

ant

walking stick

grasshopper

dragonfly

caterpillar

I am brown. I look like a stick.

I am small and yellow. I can sting. I make honey.

I am large. I have strong clear wings. I eat insects.

I have strong legs. I can hop. I eat insects.

I live in a colony underground.

I am long. I turn into a butterfly.

Objective: To learn that insects live where there is food, water, and natural protection from enemies.

Insect Homes

Do you know where insects live? ■ They live just about everywhere! Insects live in the grass, in trees, and in bushes. They live in the soil, under rotting leaves, in ponds, and even in your home and school. But how does an insect choose a place to live?

■ Some insects are like people: they don't like to live alone. As people live in cities, for example, ants live in *colonies*. Ants dig underground tunnels for their colonies to live in. Although these ant cities are often very large, the only part we can see is a tiny hill on top of the ground. Have you ever seen an anthill?

■ Bees and wasps also live together, but they build their homes off the ground. Bees live in homes that are called *hives*. Bees make their hives out of wax. Wasps also live in hives, but they use wood to build with. Each tiny piece of wood used in the hive has been chewed up by a wasp!

Of course, not all insects live together with others of their kind. Most insects live any place in which they can find food, safety, and a good spot to lay their eggs. A mosquito needs water in which to lay its eggs, so mosquitoes live around lakes or ponds. Fleas and ticks need to be near warm-blooded animals, such as dogs and mice. Do you know why? [Ticks and fleas get their food—blood—from warm-blooded animals.] ■ A caterpillar lives where there

are lots of leaves to eat. Termites lay their eggs in rotting wood and they like to eat wood. So they live in old wet logs or in houses! A cockroach can eat almost anything and can lay its eggs almost anywhere. So where do you think cockroaches live? (everywhere!)

■ Insects choose places to live where they can be safe and eat well. Are people like that? ■ Do you have food, water, and a safe place to live in? ■ What else do you have?

ant colony

Vocabulary

larva (plural, larvae)—a baby insect, just hatched from an egg, that does not look like its parents. All larvae become pupae before reaching adulthood.

pupa (plural, pupae)—the time in an insect's development between larva and adult. In the pupa stage, the insect does not move or eat.

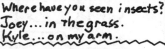

❏ Insect Survey

Ask children where they have seen insects. Record their responses on experience chart paper and discuss.

❏ Ant Farm Activity

Purchase a giant ant farm and set it up in your science center. (See *Resources*, page 18.) Have children work at the ant farm in pairs. Ask each pair to observe the farm. Discuss what the children see. Then have children take photographs of the ants at work or draw pictures of what they've seen. Ask youngsters to dictate stories about their observations which you can attach to their photographs or art work. Display finished pieces.

❏ Anatomy of a Bee

Use the picture on page 17 as a guide for drawing a large bee on oaktag. Label the parts of the bee. Make a copy of page 17 and white out the labels. Then make a number of copies of the picture without labels and place them in the science center. Have children label the parts of the bee. [Have younger children count the body parts and say their names. Then have them color the picture.]

❏ Imaginary Insects

Once children have learned the characteristics of real insects, have them create imaginary ones. Use these directions as imagination starters:

☐ Draw or write about an insect that lives in water, in a cave, in snow, in your house, or on the moon.

☐ Draw an insect you would like to have as a pet.

☐ Tell where your imaginary insect lives, what it eats, and anything else that makes it special. [For example, "It has red-striped legs. It has purple eyes!"]

❏ Honey From the Bees

Have on hand several kinds of honey—light, dark, flavored—and crackers. Explain that only honeybees make honey. Ask children to taste each kind of honey, one at a time, on a cracker. Which one did they like best? What were the differences between the kinds of honey?

❏ Insect Collection

You need: a clear, wide-mouthed, plastic container with a lid

Take children on an insect hunt. Remind youngsters not to pick up insects with their hands unless they *know* they are harmless. Crickets, butterflies, and moths are okay to handle. Collect one insect at a time. Take the trapped animal back to the classroom and let the children observe it with a magnifying glass. Discuss their observations. Release the insect. On another day, find another kind of insect to observe.

❏ A Dragonfly Poem

Teach this delightful poem to your children. Copy it on chart paper. As you say each word in the poem, point to the word on the chart. Let children draw pictures around the poem.

She lives near the pond
Where the cattails are high,
And the frogs on the lily pads
Croak and say, "Hi!"

"Play with us, dragonfly.
"Don't be so shy."
"Thank you," she drones,
"But I must say good-bye."

Then she flutters her wings
Until they are dry,
And she takes to the air—
Up into the sky.

Science Sheet Notes

Where Do I Live?, page 28—Give children this sheet to complete after they have listened to the story on page 26.

Where Do I Live?

Draw a line from each insect to its home. [See page 27.]

Objective: To learn about the stages insects go through to reach adulthood.

How Do I Look?

Do you know how insects have babies? ■ Almost all insects hatch from eggs. Many insects do not look like their parents when they hatch. Instead, they look like little white worms. These baby insects are called *larvae*. [Can you say lar-vī?] Larvae don't have wings, and often they don't have legs. So how do they grow up to look like their parents? ■ Well, they do something fantastic! They change shape!

Insects go through something called *metamorphosis*. That's just a big word that means they change shape. People can grow bigger or fatter, but they always stay the same shape. They have two arms, two legs, and one head. But certain insects—flies, wasps, moths, and butterflies—are born looking like worms!

These larvae start to eat lots of food as soon as they are born. They grow quickly. After a while, they stop eating and seem to fall into a deep sleep as their bodies use the food to change from the worm shape into the shape of their parents' bodies. The baby insects are called *pupae* (pu-pī) while they sleep. Can you imagine how it would feel to go to sleep looking one way and wake up looking completely different? ■ Well, that's what happens to the insects while they are pupae!

Not all insects go through this sleeping time. When some baby insects—such as dragonflies and grasshoppers—are born, they do look like their parents, except they don't have wings. These babies are called *nymphs* instead of larvae. Nymphs never go through the sleeping time. They don't have to go to sleep to change shape, because they already look like their parents.

If you could go through metamorphosis, what shape would you like to become?

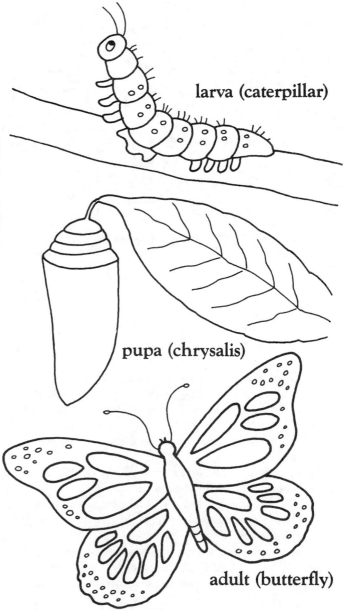

larva (caterpillar)

pupa (chrysalis)

adult (butterfly)

Vocabulary

metamorphosis—a process through which an insect changes from one shape into another. Complete metamorphosis involves four stages: egg, larva, pupa, adult. Incomplete metamorphosis involves three stages: egg, nymph, adult.

larva (plural, larvae)—a baby insect, just hatched from an egg, that does not look like its parents; all larvae become pupae before reaching adulthood.

pupa (plural, pupae)—the time in an insect's development between larva and adult. In the pupa stage, the insect does not move or eat.

nymph—a baby insect that looks like its parents and will *not* go through a pupa stage.

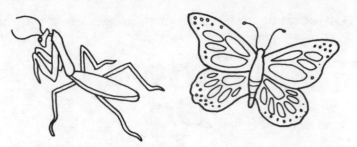

☐ Watch Mealworms Grow!

You need: mealworms
large, clear jar
oatmeal
potato or apple
cheesecloth and rubber band
chart paper and marker
magnifying glass

1 Mealworms are the larvae of darkling beetles. They can be purchased in pet stores, where they are often stocked as feed for other animals, or from Carolina Biological Supply. [See *Resources*, page 18.]

2 Fill the jar with oatmeal and add a slice of potato or apple for moisture.

3 Drop the mealworms into the jar. Cover the top of the jar with a piece of cheesecloth and a rubber band.

4 Inspect the jar every day. It can take up to four months for the larvae to change into pupae. [In the pupa stage, the mealworm is often stiff and white.]

5 Make an observation chart, such as the one shown, to hang near your specimen. Record changes as they are noted. Be sure to keep a hand magnifier near the jar at all times.

☐ Hatchling Checklist

✔Praying mantises go through incomplete metamorphosis. Purchase praying mantis egg sacs from Insect Lore Products (see *Resources*, page 18) and hatch them in your classroom.

✔Butterflies and moths go through complete metamorphosis. Order larvae from Insect Lore Products or Carolina Biological Supply (see *Resources*, page 18).

☐ Beetle Song to Grow On

Teach children this song about metamorphosis. Sing it to the tune of "Yankee Doodle."

Great big beetle lays her eggs.
Eggs hatch into larvae.
Larva grows and grows and grows,
And then sleeps as a pupa.

Pupa is a sleepy head—
Just can't seem to wake up.
Finally, he shows his head,
And now he is a grown-up ... beetle!

☐ Baby Names

Explain that just as baby dogs are called puppies and baby chickens are called chicks, some baby insects have special names. Teach the children these three:
☐ Baby fly is a *maggot*.
☐ Baby beetle is a *grub*.
☐ Baby moth or butterfly is a *caterpillar*.

Science Sheet Notes

Metamorphosis, page 31—Give each child a copy of this page to complete after the children have listened to the story on page 29. Review the stages the insects go through as children work on the sheets. Have children color the pictures once they are placed in order on a long strip of paper.

Name _____

Metamorphosis

Cut along the dotted lines. Paste the boxes in order on a long sheet of paper. [See page 30.]

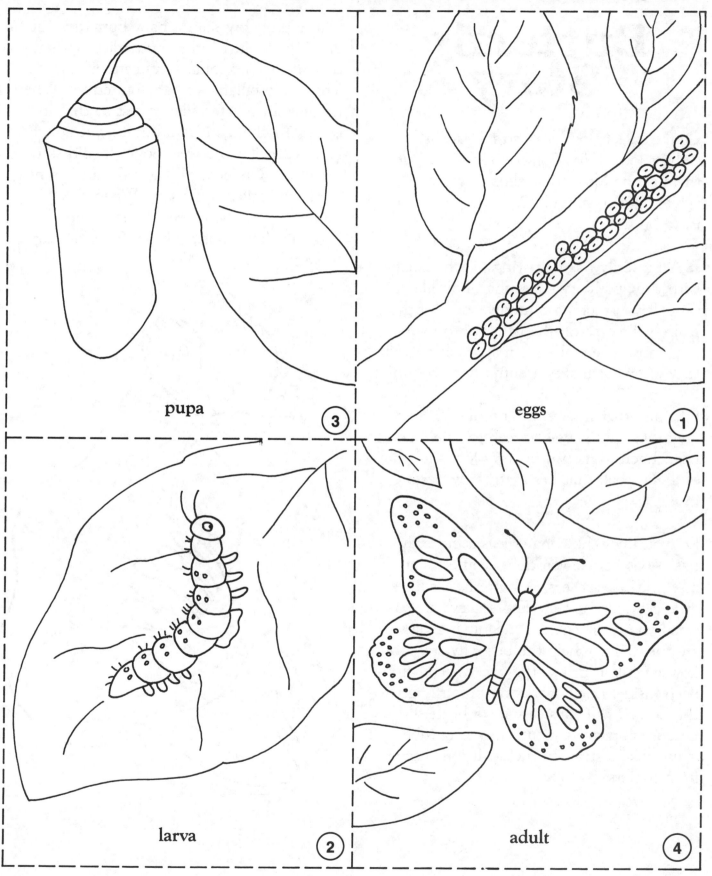

pupa ③

eggs ①

larva ②

adult ④

Objective: To learn about the butterfly's anatomy and life cycle.

Butterfly Story

Some insects look very strange to us. Others look scary. Some look funny. But there is one insect that almost everyone agrees looks beautiful. Can you guess what it is? (a butterfly)

■ A butterfly has four wings, each covered with tiny, powdery scales that look like fine dust. If you touch a butterfly, some of those scales will come off the wings onto your fingertips. The scales are many colors, and they are what makes a butterfly so beautiful.

Like all other insects, a butterfly has two antennae that it uses to feel, to smell, and to hear. Each of its two big eyes looks like half of a glass ball that has many tiny parts inside.

Do you know how many legs a butterfly has? ■ Of course you do! Because it's an insect, it has six legs. A butterfly also has little claws on its feet. Those claws are so small you would need a magnifying glass to see them. They help the butterfly stand on a flower while it drinks the sweet nectar from deep inside. But how does a butterfly get to the nectar? ■ That's easy for a butterfly because part of its mouth is a long tube that it uses like a straw to suck delicious nectar from flowers.

You've probably seen a baby butterfly, but didn't know it! Mother butterflies lay eggs that hatch into long, fuzzy caterpillars. These caterpillars are baby butterflies. When it's time for a caterpillar to rest so that its body can change into a butterfly, it attaches itself with silk to a tree. Soon, its old skin comes off. Underneath the old skin is a new, hard skin called a *chrysalis*. When the butterfly is ready, it breaks out of the chrysalis. It is finally a beautiful, grown-up butterfly!

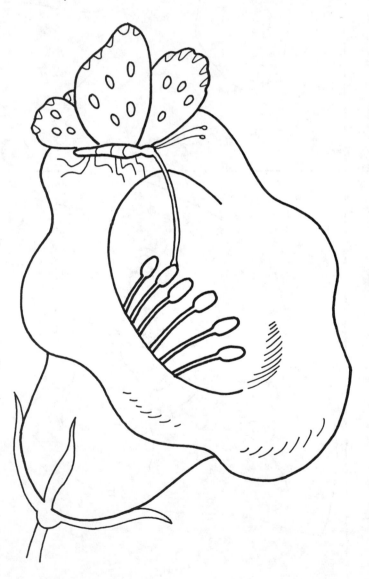

Vocabulary

caterpillar—the worm-like larva of a butterfly or moth
chrysalis—the smooth, hard case that a caterpillar is encased in during the pupa stage of its metamorphosis
nectar—a sweet liquid inside of a flower that bees and other insects drink
proboscis—the long, curled-up mouth tube that a butterfly uses to suck nectar out of flowers
pollination—the transfer of the yellow dust called pollen from one flower to another. Pollen is necessary to help flowers make seeds.

❑ Eyes-On!

"Eyes-on" is the next best thing to hands-on! Order a butterfly garden or a live butterfly culture from Insect Lore or Carolina Biological (see *Resources*, page 18). These items will allow your class to observe the various stages in the complete metamorphosis of butterflies. Make a *countdown calendar* to count the number of days it takes from chrysalis to butterfly.

❑ Spreading Pollen

1 Explain that butterflies (along with bees) are primarily responsible for pollination, the transfer of pollen from one flower to another. When a butterfly sips nectar from a flower, it steps in the flower's pollen—which is a fine, yellow dust. Then the butterfly flies to the next flower where the pollen may come off its feet. The pollen helps the new flower make seeds which are necessary for new plants to grow.
2 Sprinkle baby powder on the floor (or outdoors). Have children walk through it in their bare feet (or with shoes). Have them observe how their feet carry the powder. Explain that this is how butterflies carry pollen to help produce new plants.

❑ Nectar Drinking Time

You need: straws
         paper cup for each child
         honey-sweetened milk
         tissue paper flowers

1 Before this activity begins, pour the honey-sweetened milk to the quarter or halfway point in each cup. Put each cup on a table and surround the cups with tissue paper flowers.
2 Explain that a butterfly has a long, curled-up tube, called a *proboscis*, that it uses to suck nectar from flowers.
3 Give each child a straw and direct him or her to a honey-milk cup. Ask the children to use their proboscises to suck nectar from the flowers!

❑ Paper-Towel Butterflies

You need: white paper towels
         tray
         eyedroppers
         red, yellow, blue, and green food coloring
         clothes pins
         glue
         craft eyes
         tape
         pipe cleaners

1 Spread paper towels on a tray. Use the eyedropper to drop various colors of food coloring onto the towels. Let the towels dry.
2 Clip each dry towel in the middle, as shown, with a clothes pin. Add two craft eyes to the top of the clothes pin. Use pipe cleaners to form antennae on the clothes pin. Display finished butterflies around the room.

❑ How a Butterfly Grows

Teach this song to the tune of "The Farmer in the Dell." As you sing, have children pantomime the actions described by the words.

The butterfly lays her eggs.
The butterfly lays her eggs.
Hi ho the derrio,
The butterfly lays her eggs.

Continue singing, substituting each of the following lines for the first, second, and fourth lines of the verse above:

The caterpillar hatches out.
The caterpillar eats the leaves.
The caterpillar gets sleepy.
The caterpillar becomes a chrysalis.
The butterfly pops out.
The butterfly flies away.

❑ Butterfly Checklist

✔ Make tissue paper flowers. Drop them on the floor and have children delicately fly from one to another, spreading pollen and drinking nectar.
✔ Make caterpillar sock puppets by stuffing long, clean socks with old stockings or quilt batting. Tie segments off with yarn. Add craft eyes and pipe cleaner antennae.
✔ Buy and display butterfly posters—or make your own.

Science Sheet Notes

Butterfly, page 34—After children have listened to the story on page 32, give them this picture to color. Help them use the key and explain that butterflies often have the same color pattern on opposite wings.

Butterfly

Follow the color key as you color this picture. [See page 33.]

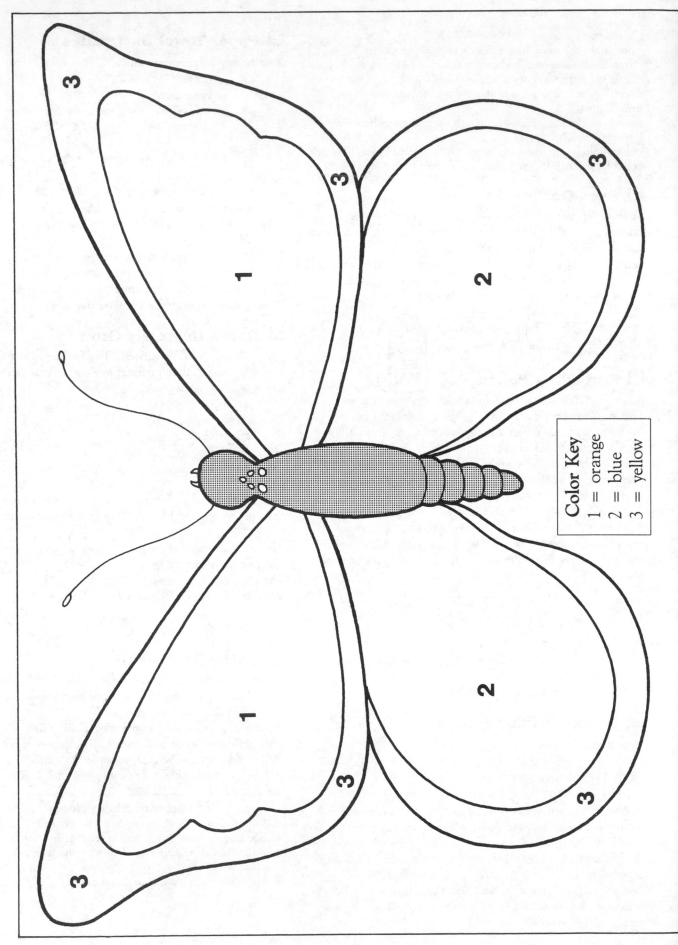

Color Key
1 = orange
2 = blue
3 = yellow

Spiders

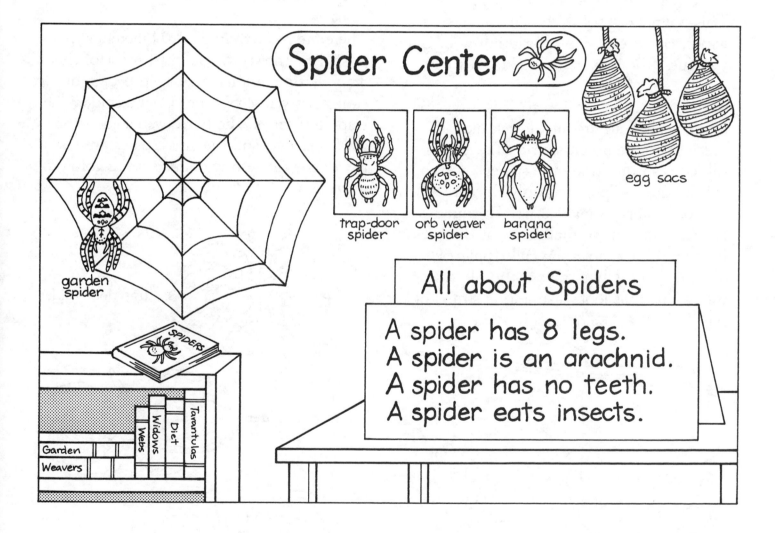

Spider Center

trap-door spider

orb weaver spider

banana spider

egg sacs

garden spider

SPIDERS

Garden Weavers · Webs · Widows · Diet · Tarantulas

All about Spiders

A spider has 8 legs.
A spider is an arachnid.
A spider has no teeth.
A spider eats insects.

Objective: To learn the parts of a spider's body and to learn that spiders are not insects.

What Are Spiders?

I know an animal that has eight legs—four legs on one side of its body and four legs on the other side. [How much is four plus four?] This animal cannot fly because it has no wings. But it can spin a beautiful web. Can you guess the animal's name? (spider!)

■ A spider is not an insect. It is a type of animal called an *arachnid* (a-rak-nid). It's special because it can spin a silk web. The silk comes from inside the spider's body, and it is a liquid—like water, only thicker. When a spider wants to make a web, it squeezes the silk out of two small holes at the back of its body. These holes are called *spinnerets*. The moment it hits the air, the silk dries into a line that looks like a long strand of hair.

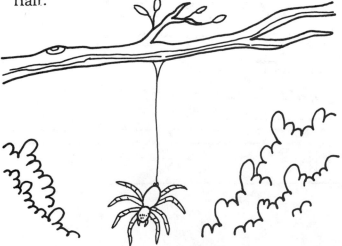

Many spiders use their silk webs to catch food. Tiny animals get stuck in the webs because the silk is sticky. Other spiders use silk as draglines. They let out long lines of silk and hang onto them as the wind blows them through the air. The spider can always crawl back up the silk line if it is blown some place it doesn't want to be!

Here's a riddle: What has eight eyes but cannot see very well? (spider) ■ Most spiders have eight eyes, although some have four or six eyes. Even with so many eyes, most spiders cannot see very well.

There are more than 30,000 different types of spiders known to scientists! Most of them are very tiny animals that help people by eating pesty insects. The banana spider, the trap-door spider, the purse web spider, the garden spider, and the grass spider are just a few of the interesting animals we're going to learn about.

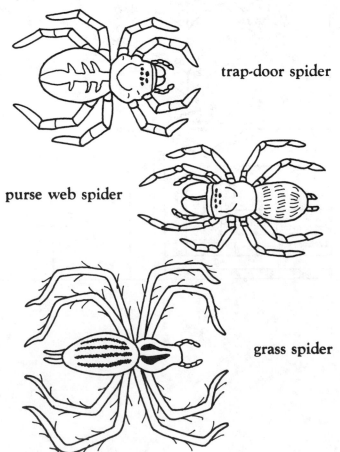

trap-door spider

purse web spider

grass spider

The Banana Spider

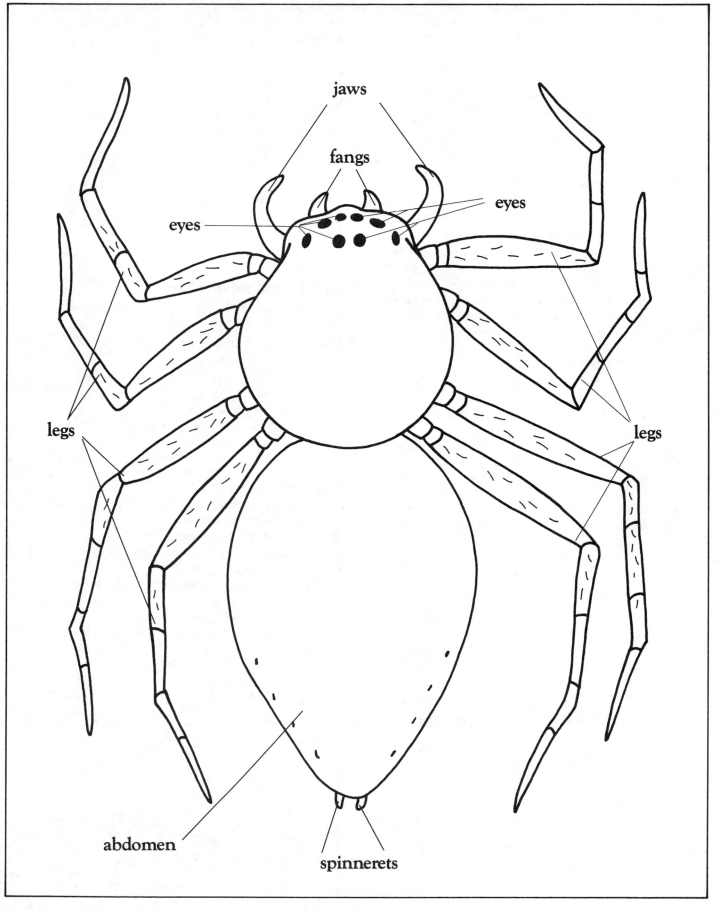

jaws

fangs

eyes

eyes

legs

legs

abdomen

spinnerets

Vocabulary

arachnid—a group of animals that includes spiders. Scorpions, daddy longlegs, and ticks are some of the other kinds of arachnids.

spinnerets—small tubes, at the back of a spider's abdomen, through which silk passes from the spider's body.

venom—a poison that kills or paralyzes its victims. Spiders can inject venom through their fangs when they attack prey.

dragline—a spider's silk line. The spider travels through the air, powered by the wind, as it clings to its dragline. The dragline is often attached to a leaf, a branch, or other lofty object.

☐ Spider Anatomy

1 Draw a large version of the picture on page 37 onto oaktag. Label the spider parts.
2 Make a copy of page 37 for each child.
3 Point to each part of the spider on the oaktag and read the labels. Ask children to color each part of the spider on their pages a different color. For example: legs=green; abdomen=blue; jaws=yellow; fangs=red; and eyes=orange.
4 Have children write their names on their pages, and then hang the colored spiders in the spider center.

☐ The Itsy Bitsy Spider

Children love this finger play song!

The itsy bitsy spider   [Wiggle fingers as you bring
Went up the water spout.   hands up in the air.]

Down came the rain,   [Move hands down, wiggling
And washed the spider out.   fingers to show rain.]

Out came the sun   [Touch hands above head;
And dried up all the rain,   then open arms down to
                                     show sunshine.]

And the itsy bitsy spider   [Wiggle fingers as you bring
Went up the spout again.   hands up in the air again.]

☐ Itsy Bitsy's House

You need: masking tape
            knife or scissors
            medium-sized cereal box
            primary color paints and brushes
            black yarn

1 Tape both ends of the box closed. Then cut a window in the box, as shown.
2 Paint the outside of the cereal box and both sides of the window flaps. Let everything dry.

3 Use a sharp pencil to punch a hole through the top of the box. Slip one end of a long piece of yarn through the hole.
4 Color and cut out the spider on this page. Staple the spider to the end of the yarn that is inside the box.
5 If you have each child make a box, let children name the spider and paint its name on the box. Other decorations may be added as desired.
6 Sing "Itsy Bitsy Spider" and have children move their spiders up and down by pulling on the yarn.

☐ Giant Spider Web

Make this giant web (approximately 4′×4′) in your classroom!

You need: ball of twine and scissors
            masking tape
            paper spider cutouts

1 Tape the end of the twine to the top of a blank wall. Move left as you let out more twine. About a foot from the first tape, tape the twine to the wall again. Continue moving left and taping, as shown, until you have an outer border. When you reach your starting point again, cut the twine.
2 Make a twine cross in the center of the outer border. The ends of the cross should intersect the tape points, as shown. Then connect the other tape points that are opposite each other with lengths of twine.
3 Add a smaller border pattern to the web, about 12″ in from the outer border. Then make another border inside of that. Be sure your tape is secure.
4 Hang paper spiders on your web. Happy Halloween!

Science Sheet Notes

Who Does Not Belong?, page 39—Remind children that spiders have eight legs. Then give them this sheet to complete.

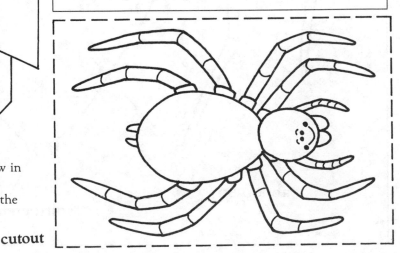

cutout

Who Does Not Belong?

Count the legs on the animals in this picture. Circle and color only the spiders. [See page 38.]

Objective: To learn the kinds of foods that spiders eat.

Breakfast with a Spider

A spider spends most of its time looking for food. What would you feed a spider if you invited it to your house for breakfast? ■ Insects would be a good choice, because spiders eat mostly insects.

But how do spiders catch insects? ■ Most of them use their webs, of course! A spider's web is like its very own supermarket. After the spider builds the web, insects may get stuck in the silk. The spider then goes "shopping" in its web to see what it has captured!

All spiders can make silk, but only some spiders use silk to spin webs. The garden spider is a good web maker; it likes to weave webs indoors and out. The orb weaver spider is the best web maker of all. It spins a web and waits in the middle of it for food to come along.

Other spiders are hunters. They don't make webs. A jumping spider can jump a long way to land on its prey. The wolf spider is a fast runner that likes to leap on top of insects before it eats them. The trap-door spider fools its prey by digging a hole and hiding inside it. When an insect comes by, the spider swings open the door covering the hole, grabs the insect, and eats it! The

banana spider is another fast runner. It loves to eat tasty cockroaches.

A spider has no teeth, so it cannot chew. How do you think spiders eat? ■ A spider grabs an insect with its powerful jaws and then injects the insect with venom. Venom is a poison that turns the insect's inner body to a liquid. The spider then sucks the liquid body out of the insect's hard outer shell.

So, now that you know what a spider likes to eat, what will you serve your visiting spider for breakfast?

orb weaver

jumping spider

wolf spider

Vocabulary
prey—any animal hunted and eaten by another animal

❏ Web Hunt

Take your class on a spider web hunt. Record where you find the webs, how big they are, and what the spider that made them looks like (if possible). Ask children to go on a hunt at home or in their backyards and report back the number and locations of webs.

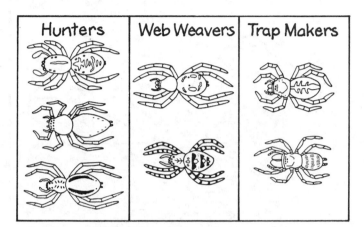

Hunters	Web Weavers	Trap Makers

❏ How Does A Spider Get Food?

1 After reading the story on page 40, give each child a copy of the spider cutouts on this page. Teach children the names of each spider. Then have them color and cut out the spiders.

2 Divide a paper-backed bulletin board into three sections, as shown. Help children place their spider cutouts in the appropriate categories.

❏ The Spider's Venom!

You need: styrofoam cup per child
sugar cube per child
very warm water

1 After reading the story on page 40, give each child a cup with several sugar cubes in the bottom. Explain that the cubes are like the inside of an insect's body—hard!

2 Have children pour a few drops of water onto the cubes. What happens? The water dissolves the sugar cubes just as the spider's venom dissolves the insect's body. Because a spider can turn its food to liquid, it can eat without chewing!

3 Discuss how people's diets would be affected if we didn't have teeth.

Science Sheet Notes

A Spider's Breakfast, page 42—After children have listened to the story on page 40, give them copies of this science sheet to complete. Remind them that most spiders eat insects.

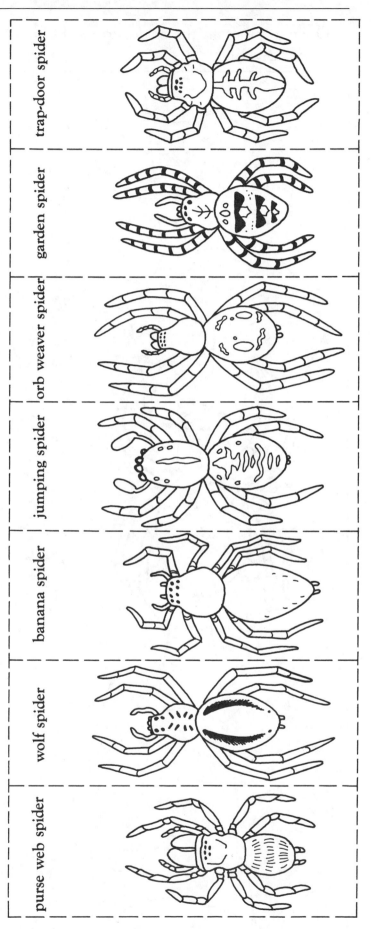

trap-door spider

garden spider

orb weaver spider

jumping spider

banana spider

wolf spider

purse web spider

41

Name _____

A Spider's Breakfast

Draw a line from the spider to all the things it will eat. Cross out the things it won't eat. [See page 41.]

Objective: To learn how spiders defend themselves from enemies.

Saved by Silk

A spider is an animal that has many enemies. Birds, insects such as wasps, snakes, lizards, frogs, and fish eat spiders. Even spiders eat spiders!

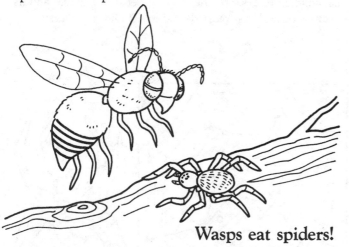

Wasps eat spiders!

A spider uses its silk lines to get away from danger. When an enemy is close by, a spider drops a long dragline from its web to the ground. The spider then slides down the dragline as if it were a rope. At the bottom, the spider jumps into the grass and hides. If a spider is up high, it can drop a dragline from a tree branch and hang in space. When the enemy leaves, the spider just climbs back up the line to safety.

dragline

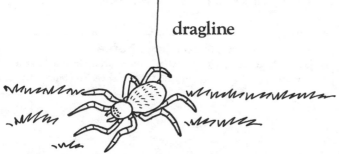

A spider usually doesn't have to worry about insects and other animals its own size. That's because a spider can hold an insect with its very powerful jaws and use venom to kill the insect. But do you think a spider can hold a dog or a bird in its jaws? (no) ■ That's right—these animals are too big for a spider to harm. The spider has to run away or hide from bigger animals.

Now, what helps spiders hide? (their colors) ■ Spiders are usually the same color as their surroundings. They blend in with the colors, so it's hard for other animals to see them. This is called *camouflage*. Brown, black, or green spiders blend in with dirt, trees, and grass. Some spiders even weave special patterns in their webs to hide behind. Camouflage is nature's very smart way of helping animals hide from enemies.

Most spiders do not harm people. However, there are two types of spiders—the black widow and the brown recluse—that are poisonous. Their bites can make a person very sick. But most spiders are afraid of people—they try to run away or hide from big giants like you and me!

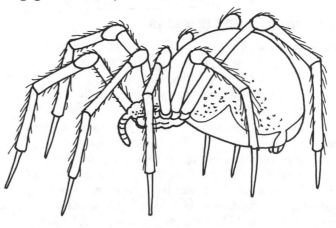

black widow

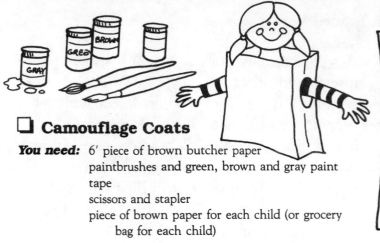

This is Charlie Spider. He is so strong that elephants are afraid of him.

Kyle

☐ Camouflage Coats

You need: 6' piece of brown butcher paper
paintbrushes and green, brown and gray paint
tape
scissors and stapler
piece of brown paper for each child (or grocery
bag for each child)
yarn

1 Divide the 6' piece of brown paper into three equal sections. Ask children to paint one section green, one brown, and the other gray. Hang the painted paper on the wall with tape.

2 Give each child a small piece of brown paper or a grocery bag. Help the child cut arm holes in the paper. Have each child choose a color (green, brown, or gray) to paint the paper. If desired, children may make colored headbands that match their vests. [Staple a 3″-wide paper strip into a circle that fits the child's head. Paint it to match the vest.]

3 Tell children to pretend they are spiders hiding in the woods. Have each child show how he or she blends with each background. Discuss camouflage with the children. "Would the brown spider be safer on the green or brown background? Would the green spider be easier to see on a leaf or on sand?" etc.

4 Let children make colored spiders to hang from yarn in front of the colored panels. Children may draw their own spiders and cut them out or use the cutouts on page 41.

☐ Camouflage Diorama

You need: paintbrushes and green, brown, blue, gray, and
black paint
shoe box per child
green, brown, blue, and gray plasticine or clay

1 Paint the inside of a shoe box the color of a spider's habitat (whether it be grass, a garden, the forest, or a sandy beach).

2 Ask each child to mold his or her own spider from plasticine or clay. The spider must match the color of the child's shoe box. [If you do not have the right colors of plasticine, have children make spiders from colored construction paper.] Have the child place the spider in the shoe box.

3 Discuss why it's difficult to find a spider when it's the same color as its environment.

☐ Super Spiders

Ask children to dictate and illustrate their own spider stories. Ask children to describe the meeting between a spider and its enemy. How did the spider defend itself? Did it get away?

☐ Pattern Spiders

Many spiders, like the garden spider, weave patterns into their webs to help them hide from enemies. Draw a web on a piece of paper and make copies of it for the children. Then ask children to draw a different web pattern on top of the copy. [They may use zigzags, stripes, dots, etc., for their patterns.] Have each child cut out a paper spider and draw on it the same pattern he or she used on the web. See how the spider blends with the web when placed on top of the paper.

Science Sheet Notes

Natural Enemies, page 45—After children have listened to the story on page 43, give them this science sheet to complete.

44

Name _____

Natural Enemies

Color the animals that would eat the spider. [See page 44.]

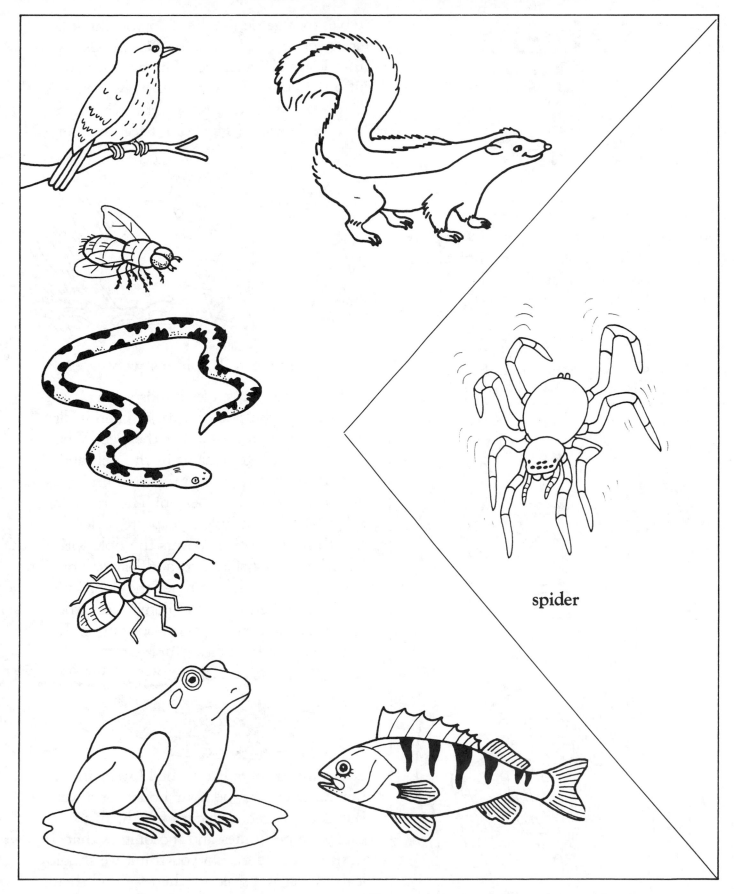

spider

45

Objective: To learn that spiders live in many different places and use webs to survive.

Where Do I Live?

Spiders live almost everywhere in the world. Some spiders live mainly in very cold places, while others live mainly in very hot places. Some spiders make their homes in dry places, and others live in very wet places.

Can you guess where a garden spider lives? (a garden) ■ That's right—a garden spider builds its web among the flowers or vege-

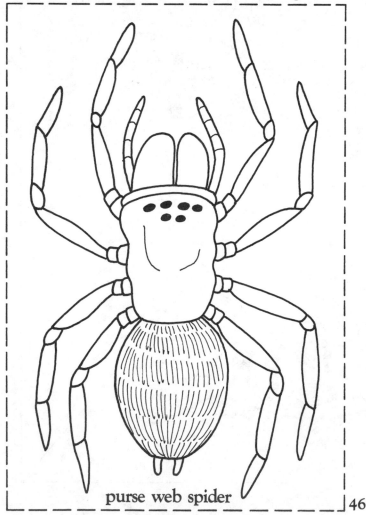

purse web spider

tables in a garden. Where do you think a grass spider lives? (in grass) ■ It builds a web that looks like a funnel. The web is woven into the grass or low bushes. Have you ever brushed against a grass spider's web when you were playing? How did it feel on your skin?

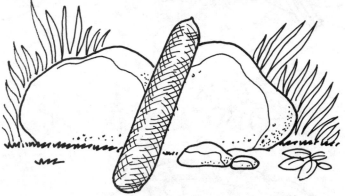

purse web spider's web

■ The purse web spider builds a long, tube-like web on the side of a rock. Then it digs a hole in the ground under the web. When careless insects get caught in the web and slide down the tube into the hole under it, they are captured and eaten! The trap-door spider also digs a hole to capture its food. But this tricky spider covers the hole with a "door" made of silk, dirt, and leaves. The trap-door spider hides under the door inside the hole. When an insect comes near, the spider opens the door and hops out, grabs the insect, and gobbles it up!

trap-door spider

Sometimes spiders like to build webs in our homes. Look around your house for a web. But don't forget, a spider's web helps to catch the pesty flies and mosquitoes that we want to get rid of. Do you think we should leave spider webs alone when we find them?

Vocabulary

funnel—a cone-shaped object with a tube at the bottom
trap door—a door that is even with the surface of the floor; usually hidden

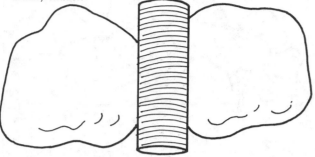

❑ Spider Web Fun!

This activity is an interesting way to experience building a web like the one made by the purse web spider.

You need: flour and water
6″ pieces of thin string
toilet paper tube
2 small, brown paper bags
newpaper and paints
copy of purse web spider from page 46 per child
copy of page 22 or 25 for each child
stapler and glue

1 Mix flour and water to make a papier mâché paste. Dip 6″ pieces of string in the paste and wrap the string around the toilet paper tube. Let dry. This is the web.
2 Stuff the bags with newpaper and staple closed. Paint them to look like round rocks.
3 Glue the rocks to the web, as shown. Give children copies of the purse web spider and insects to color and cut out. Trap insects in the web.

❑ Trap Door Traps

You need: scissors
glue and leaves
a shoe box
tracing of trap-door spider from page 41
craft sticks and yarn
copies of page 22

1 Partially cut a 3″ to 4″ circle into the side of a shoe box. Be sure to leave part of the circle connected to the box, as shown.

2 Tell children that this is similar to the trap-door spider's trap. Glue leaves on top of the door and over the rest of the side of the box.
3 Trace the trap-door spider on page 41; color the tracing; and paste it onto construction paper. Cut out the spider. Paste the cutout onto a craft stick.
4 Give children copies of page 22. Have them paste their copies onto construction paper, color the insects, and cut them out. Staple a piece of yarn to each insect.
5 Let children play in pairs or small groups. One child can dangle an insect near the trap door while another child, with the spider in wait, pops the door, and takes the insect!
6 Leave this display in your science center for hours of fun! [If desired, each child can make his or her own trap-door box.]

❑ A Spider Vivarium

Children love to observe spiders they have captured. Set up your own observation tank.

You need: soil
aquarium tank or very large jar (1 gal)
leaves, rocks, branch
small wet sponge
cheesecloth and tape
plastic container or net (for catching spiders and insects)

1 Place soil in the bottom of an aquarium tank and cover it with a few leaves, rocks, and a large branch. Place a small wet sponge in the tank for moisture.
2 Go on a spider hunt. Be sure to capture your spider with a net or plastic container so that you do not hurt it.
3 Place the spider in your tank. Cover the tank with cheesecloth. Tape the cover in place.
4 Have children observe the spider over several days. Does it move around much? Does it eat leaves? If you are lucky, the spider will spin a web on a branch.
5 Add a live insect to the tank and watch what happens.

Science Sheet Notes
Where Do I Live?, page 48—After children have listened to the story on page 46, give them this science sheet to complete.

Name _____

Where Do I Live?

Cut out each spider and glue it in its correct home. [See page 47.]

trap-door spider

garden spider

grass spider

purse web spider

Objective: To learn that mother spiders lay eggs, that baby spiders are called *spiderlings*, and that spiders grow by molting.

What Is a Spiderling?

How do you think a mother spider has babies? ■If you said, "She lays eggs," you're right! All spiders lay eggs. Because the eggs are so very tiny, the mother spider wraps all of her eggs in an *egg sac*—made from silk—to protect them and keep them from drying out. Some mother spiders die soon after they lay their eggs, but other mother spiders live and guard their eggs until the baby spiders, called *spiderlings*, hatch.

When the weather is too cold, the spiderlings stay in their egg sac until it warms up. But when the weather warms up, they tear open the sac and out they pop! A spiderling can use its spinnerets as soon as it's born. Can you tell me what spinnerets are? (the part of the spider the silk comes from)

■Often, the first thing the spiderling does is put out a silk line that it can ride the wind on while it looks for food. When a spiderling lets the wind blow it and its dragline through the air, the spider is *ballooning*. Can you guess why we call it ballooning? [Many spiders are so light that they float like balloons on a breeze while they are attached to their draglines.]

■A spiderling grows into a big spider by *molting*. That means it grows a whole new skin under its old one and then breaks out and leaves the old skin behind. A spiderling molts three or four times before it is fully grown! When a female spider is grown, she is ready to have spiderlings of her own. Most female spiders are bigger than male spiders, and both are bigger than tiny spiderlings!

Next time you go on a nature walk, be sure to look for a spider's egg sac hanging from a leaf or on the branch of a tree!

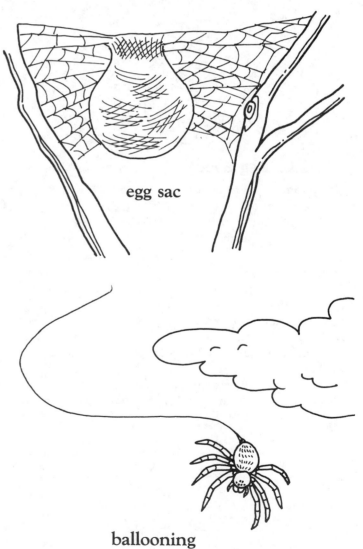

egg sac

ballooning

Vocabulary

egg sac—a small case, made of silk, spun by a mother spider to hold all of her eggs

ballooning—a method of travel used by spiders

molt—When an animal sheds its skin because a new skin has grown under the old, we say that the animal has molted. Some animals molt as they grow.

spiderling—the name for a baby spider; applies to period between hatching and adulthood

❑ The Spider's Cocoon

After reading "What Is a Spiderling?" on page 49, compare the way a spider weaves a silk case around its eggs to protect them and the way a caterpillar makes a cocoon around itself. Point out that the egg case is like a nursery where baby spiders, once they hatch, can live until it's safe to go outside. A caterpillar's cocoon is used to protect the caterpillar while its body changes shape (to become a butterfly).

❑ Make Egg Sacs

You need: white tissue paper
water
yarn or string and tacks
pencil and paper

1 Have each child make his or her own tiny spider "eggs" by rolling small pieces of wet tissue paper into balls. Let dry.
2 Wrap the "eggs" in a large piece of tissue to keep them together. Wrap yarn around and around the tissue until the tissue is completely covered.
3 Attach a long piece of yarn to the sac. Hang all the sacs from the ceiling (use tacks) in your spider center or around the room.
4 Have each child write or dictate a story about his or her spiderlings. Ask the children, "What type of spiders are in your egg sac? When will the spiders hatch? How big will they grow?"

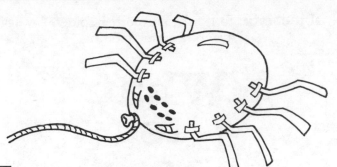

❑ Spiderling Balloons

You need: medium-sized balloon per child
masking tape
8 2"×4" construction paper legs per child
black markers
yarn or string

1 Help children blow up their balloons.
2 Make a sample *spiderling balloon* to show children how to tape four construction paper legs to one side of the spider balloon and four to the other side.
3 Add eight dots for eyes and two lines for jaws with your black marker.
4 Tie yarn or string onto each spiderling balloon and take the balloons outside. Have children release them in a gentle breeze so they can watch the spiderlings go ballooning! [Be sure that the string is long enough for a child to grab it quickly if necessary.]

❑ Spider Checklist

✔ Read the story or watch the videotape of *Charlotte's Web*. Discuss why Charlotte needs to find a place to lay her eggs. Have children illustrate their favorite parts of the story.
✔ Have children cut out big spiders (mothers), smaller spiders (fathers), and tiny spiders (spiderlings) from construction paper. Glue each set of cutouts onto a piece of paper and write spider family stories!

Science Sheet Notes

Spider Minibook, page 51—Remind children that baby spiders can make silk as soon as they hatch. Then give them this sheet to complete.

Name _____

Spider Minibook

Color the pictures. Cut them out. Put them in order. Staple pages together to make a book. [See page 50.]

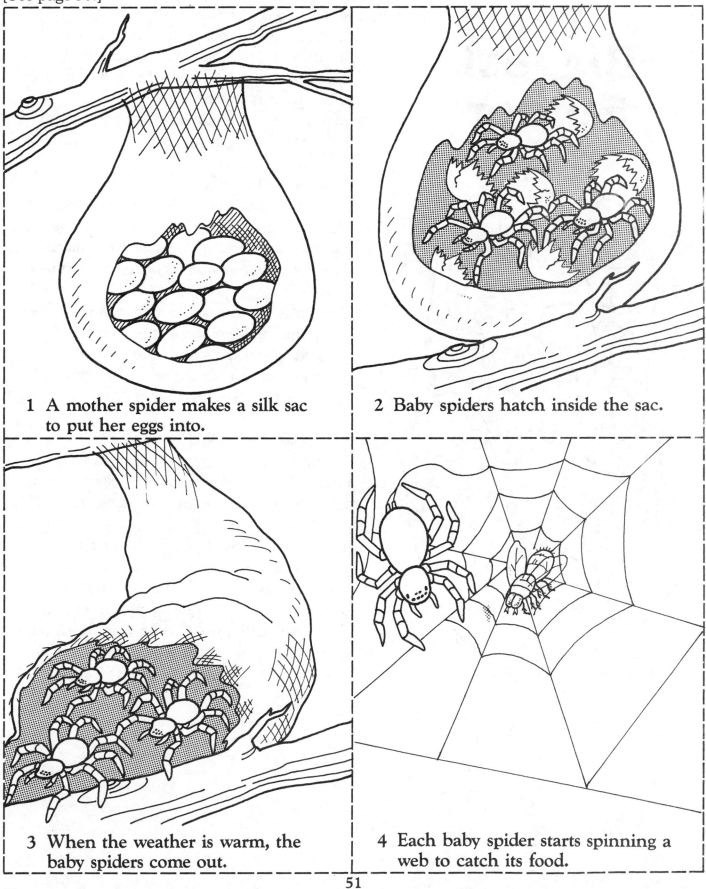

1 A mother spider makes a silk sac to put her eggs into.

2 Baby spiders hatch inside the sac.

3 When the weather is warm, the baby spiders come out.

4 Each baby spider starts spinning a web to catch its food.

Objective: To learn about tarantulas.

The Biggest Spider

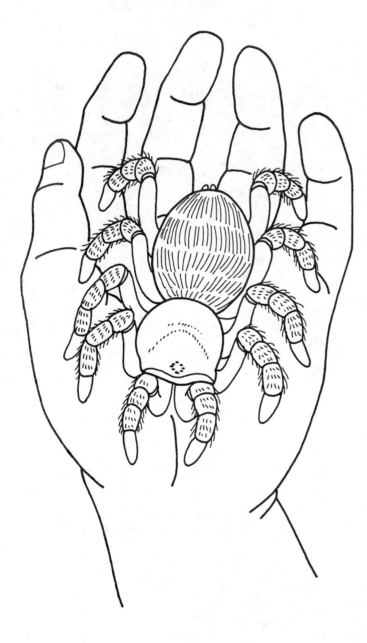

There is a spider that is so big that people think it must be poisonous and dangerous. But it isn't! This spider can stretch itself as long as ten inches. That's almost as long as a ruler, and it is much larger than most spiders. Have you guessed the name of this spider yet? It's a tarantula!

A tarantula looks very soft and furry because unlike most spiders, it has hair. Most tarantulas live in holes or under rocks, and they are *nocturnal* animals; that means they only come out at night to find food.

Tarantulas eat lots of different animals. They eat beetles and grasshoppers, spiders and millipedes, and frogs and toads. Some tarantulas are so big that they can even eat small birds, snakes, and lizards!

Most spiders only live for one or two years, but tarantulas live much longer. In fact, it takes many kinds of tarantulas eight to ten years just to become grown-up spiders.

Tarantulas are not fast runners or high jumpers, so they can't get away very fast. They are easy to tame. Some tarantulas make great pets, and many people keep them in their homes. Would you like to have a pet tarantula? Where would you keep it?

A Pet Tarantula

[See page 54.]

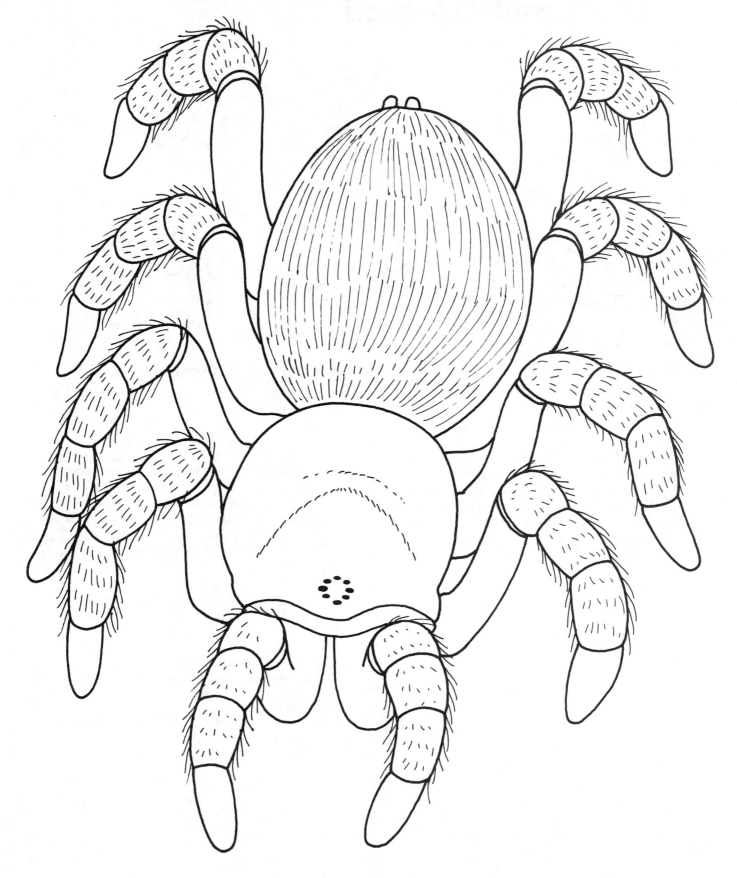

53

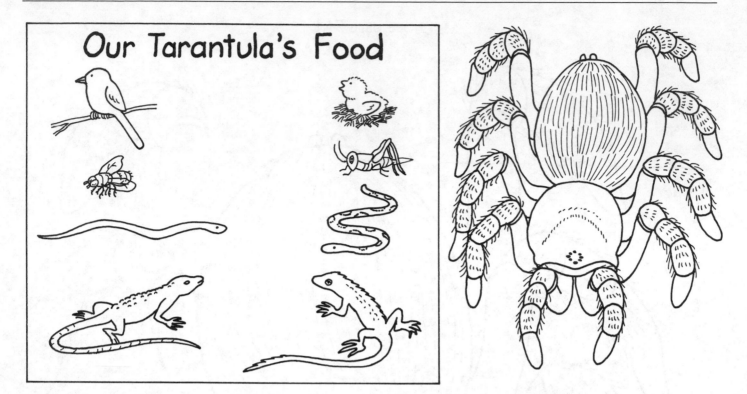

Our Tarantula's Food

❏ Giant Spider

Make your own classroom tarantula!

You need: large piece of white oaktag
black, wide-tipped marker
glue
2″ pieces of brown and black yarn

1 Enlarge the spider from page 53 onto oaktag.
2 Ask children to glue yarn "hair" all over the spider's body.
3 Hang the spider in your spider center. Have children cut out pictures of birds and snakes (from copies of other pages in this book or from magazines) and paste them on a chart entitled, *Our Tarantula's Food.*

❏ A Tarantula Cinquain

Here's a formula for writing cinquains and a sample one about tarantulas.

Cinquain Formula

1st line = 1 word, the name of the animal
2nd line = 2 words, to describe the animal
3rd line = 3 words, to describe the animal's actions
4th line = 4 words, to describe your feelings about it
5th line = 1 word, the group the animal belongs in

Tarantula Cinquain

Tarantula
Big, hairy
Hiding, hunting, stretching
Scared silly, really worried
Spider

Science Sheet Notes

A Pet Tarantula, page 53—Give each child a copy of this science sheet. Have the children color the spider, paste the sheet onto construction paper, and cut out the spider. Attach a piece of yarn to the spider's head so it can be taken for a walk, just like a dog!

Amphibians

Our Amphibian Center

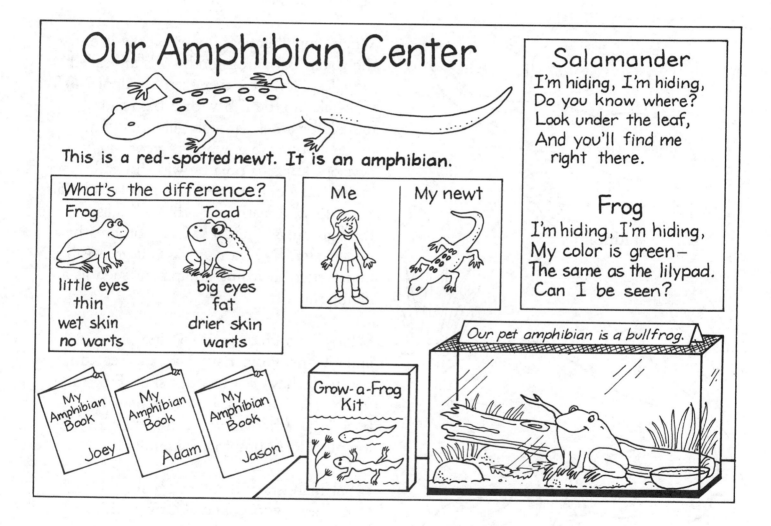

This is a red-spotted newt. It is an amphibian.

What's the difference?

Frog	Toad
little eyes	big eyes
thin	fat
wet skin	drier skin
no warts	warts

Me	My newt

Salamander

I'm hiding, I'm hiding,
Do you know where?
Look under the leaf,
And you'll find me
right there.

Frog

I'm hiding, I'm hiding,
My color is green—
The same as the lilypad.
Can I be seen?

My Amphibian Book — Joey

My Amphibian Book — Adam

My Amphibian Book — Jason

Grow-a-Frog Kit

Our pet amphibian is a bullfrog.

Objective: To learn what amphibians look like and that they live part of their lives in water and part on land.

Is This an Amphibian?

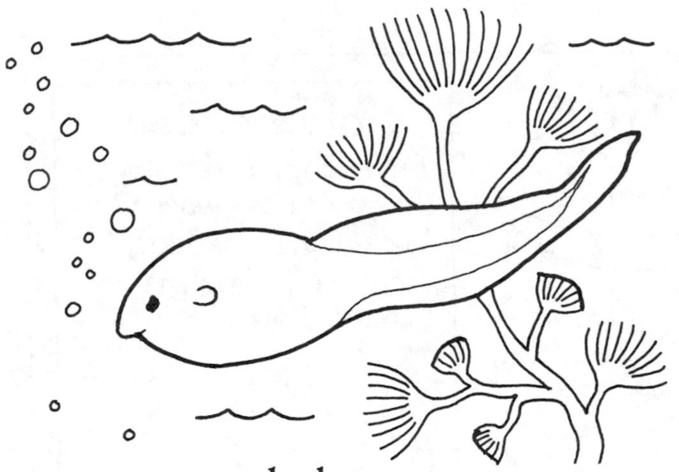

tadpole

frog

Some animals, like fish, need to live in the water all their lives because that's where they breathe. Other animals, like birds and insects, need to live on land all their lives in order to breathe. Only one kind of animal can breathe in *water* for part of its life, and on *land* for another part of it. Do you know the name of this kind of animal? ■ That's right! It's an amphibian.

When amphibians are babies, they live in the water. Baby frogs and toads are called tadpoles. Have you ever seen a tadpole? ■ It looks like a little fish with a big head. A tadpole breathes through gills that grow inside its body, but when it grows up, it develops lungs to breathe with instead. Now it can come out of the water and breathe air. How do *you* breathe air—through gills or through lungs? (lungs) ■ Can you breathe underwater? [No, not unless you are wearing underwater breathing equipment such as a diving tank.]

■ Frogs and toads are two kinds of amphibians. Frogs have smooth, wet skin, and toads have bumpy, dry skin. Frogs and toads have four legs, but frogs have long back legs. What do you think they use their long legs for? (jumping, swimming)

■ Salamanders and newts are amphibians too. They are long and skinny, with a tail and four short legs. Their legs are not good for jumping, but they are good for moving fast along the ground.

Some amphibians make good pets. They are fun to watch and easy to care for. Would you like a pet frog or salamander?

56

Amphibians

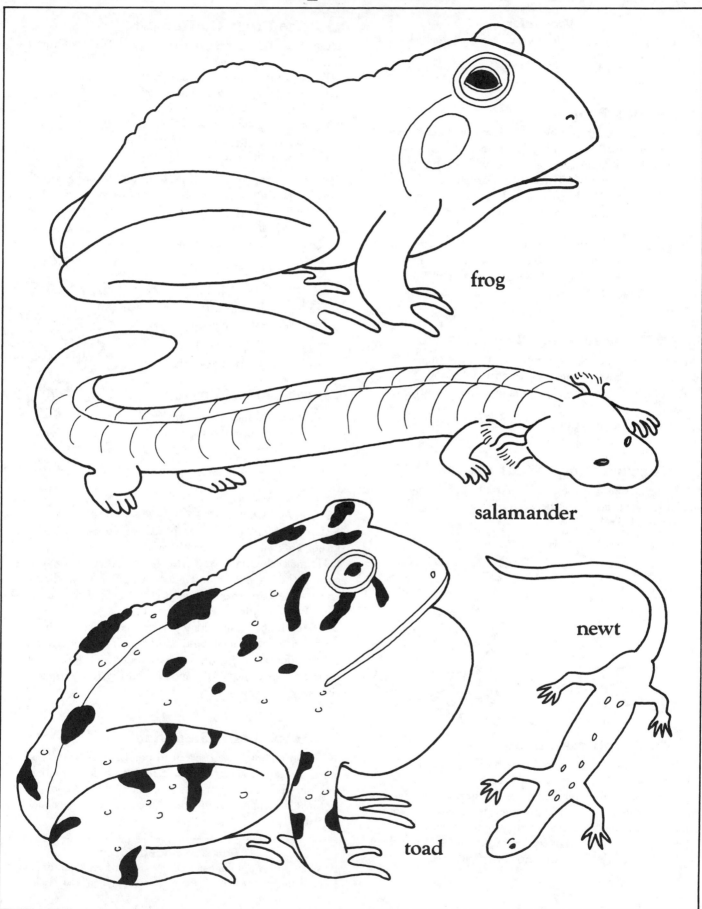

frog

salamander

newt

toad

Vocabulary

gills—the organs, on each side of a tadpole's head, that allow the animal to breathe while swimming in water

tadpole—a young amphibian. It lives under water and has gills, no legs, and a tail.

☐ Watch a Frog

1 Children are fascinated by tadpoles and will delight in watching this small "see-through" specimen change from tadpole to frog in approximately three weeks! Send for a "Grow-A-Frog Kit" from Three Rivers Amphibian, Inc., 668 Broadway, Dept. GG, Massapequa, N.Y. 11758. The kit includes a tadpole, a plex-aquarium, and a Fun & Fact Booklet.

2 If you order more than one tadpole at a time, you can compare sizes and different stages of growth. As tadpoles grow nearer to becoming frogs, send for the small frog vivarium and food. This is the perfect amphibian project and children will love it!

☐ At Home in Your Classroom

Once you have tadpoles and frogs in class, ask small groups of children to observe them. Discuss the following:

☐ A tadpole has small eyes, a long tail, and smooth, moist skin.

☐ An adult frog has strong, webbed hind legs and a long sticky tongue.

☐ What's a Frog? What's a Toad?

Read *Frog and Toad Are Friends* by Arnold Lobel. Discuss the similarities and differences between frogs and toads. Write an experience chart.

Frog
little eyes
thin, wet skin
no warts

Toad
big eyes
fat, drier skin
warts

☐ My Amphibian Book

Children love to "read" books they have made. Photocopy four sheets of paper for each child, each with a different sentence about amphibian characteristics printed at the bottom. Have children illustrate their pages. Staple a cover entitled *My Amphibian Book* to the front of each book. Display in your amphibian section. Ask children to read the books aloud to the class and show their pictures.

☐ "The Frogs Go Hopping"

Teach this delightful song to the tune of "When Johnny Comes Marching Home."

The frogs go hopping one by one, hurrah, hurrah,
The frogs go hopping one by one, hurrah, hurrah,
The frogs go hopping one by one,
The little one stops to suck its thumb,
And they all go hopping down into the pond,
To get out of the rain.

[Repeat the song for two, three, four, and five frogs by substituting the correct numbers in lines 1 and 2, and the following words for lines 3 and 4.]

The frogs go hopping two by two,
The little one stops to tie its shoe,

The frogs go hopping three by three,
The little one fell and skinned its knee,

The frogs go hopping four by four,
The little one stops to shut the door,

The frogs go hopping five by five,
The little one stops to touch the hive,

☐ Egg-Carton Frogs

You need: cardboard egg cartons
paintbrushes
green paint
glue
craft eyes
scissors
red and green construction paper

1 Give each child half a cardboard egg carton to paint green. This will be the frog's body.

2 To make the frog's head, attach two individual egg carton cups to the body. [See illustration.] Children paint the heads green. When dry, they glue craft eyes onto the egg carton cups. Place each frog head onto its body.

3 For each child, cut a long piece of red construction paper in the shape of a tongue and two longer pieces of green construction paper in the shape of frogs' legs. Children glue a tongue to the center of the mouth and legs to the bottom of the body.

☐ Amphibian Checklist

✔ Go on an amphibian search in ponds, lakes, and wooded areas. Bring binoculars and containers to hold amphibians.

✔ Visit your pet store or local zoo's amphibian section.

✔ Make an amphibian vivarium. Include newts, salamanders, and frogs.

Science Sheet Notes

What Are Amphibians?, page 59—Remind children that amphibians breathe in the water as tadpoles and on land as adults. Then give them this science sheet to complete.

Name _____

What Are Amphibians?

Color the amphibians that have tails *red*. Color the amphibians with no tails *green*.
[See page 58.]

Objective: To learn that tadpoles eat underwater plants and tiny animals, and that adult amphibians only eat tiny animals.

What Do Amphibians Eat?

Do you remember what some baby amphibians are called? ■ That's right, they're tadpoles. Tadpoles live in quiet ponds and streams. As soon as they hatch from eggs, tadpoles find underwater plants to hold onto with their mouths. They can eat the plants and stay in one place at the same time. Why do you think they eat like this? [They are too little to swim around in the dangerous pond. Other animals might eat them.] ■ When they are bigger, tadpoles look for their own food in the pond. They eat plants and tiny animals too.

Grown-up frogs and toads don't eat plants. They only eat tiny animals. Some of their favorite foods are insects, spiders, earthworms, and small fish. Do you know how frogs and toads catch their food? (with their long, sticky tongues) ■ A frog or toad can roll its tongue out of its mouth very quickly to catch flies. The sticky tongue comes out so fast that you can't see it. Can you move your tongue like a frog's tongue?

■ A mud puppy is a kind of large salamander. It springs quickly out of the mud to catch food. Mud puppies hunt for food early in the morning and just before the sun goes down at night. Why do you think these are

good times for mud puppies to capture food? [That's when there are lots of insects around. Also, it's safer for mud puppies to hunt when it's barely light out—they can't be seen easily by enemies.]

■ Did you know that frogs and salamanders have tiny teeth? ■ These teeth are just in the top part of their mouths—not in the bottom. They're not good for chewing, but they are good for holding food.

Amphibians are always busy looking for a tasty meal. In lakes and streams, in woods and forests, they're sure to find something good to eat!

Vocabulary

snail—a slow-moving animal (mollusk) protected by a spiral-shaped shell

slug—an animal (gastropod) that looks like a snail, with little or no shell

❑ Pet Amphibian

Bull frogs and newts make good pets because they are easy to care for.

You need: pet amphibian
terrarium
live insects
Polaroid camera

1 Keep your amphibian in a moist terrarium. [Frogs need a terrarium that is partly filled with water. You can add a plastic bowl for the water.] Include a rock and a dry area with a plant in your terrarium, and provide your amphibian with live food. Frogs and toads like to eat insects or earthworms. Newts like snails and slugs. [Amphibian food can be bought in pet stores or captured.]

2 Have children observe the amphibian when food is placed in the terrarium and at intervals over several days. Use an inexpensive Polaroid camera to photograph the amphibian as it eats. If you keep a frog or toad, children will be able to observe a) the animal's sticky tongue as it captures food, b) the way it quickly pounces on the food, and c) the food in its mouth.

3 Help children create a photo display. Invite other classes to see the pet and the photographs.

frog terrarium

newt terrarium

❑ Party Blow-outs!

You need: double-sided tape
party blower for each child
small pieces of paper

1 Talk about the sticky tongue of a toad and a frog. Discuss how the tongue helps them catch food.

2 Let children complete the "Something Sticky" science sheet on page 63.

3 Make bands of tape. Press one band against the end of each party blower. Let children experiment with the blowers to see if they can grab small pieces of paper with them.

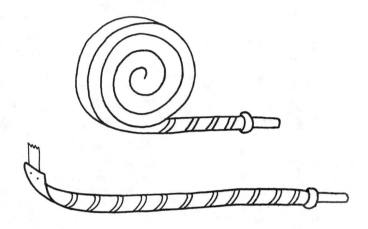

❑ Buy a Newt

Not everyone can find a newt! But you can buy one inexpensively to raise as your classroom pet. Send away to Carolina Biological Supply Company, 2700 York Road, Burlington, NC 27215-3398.

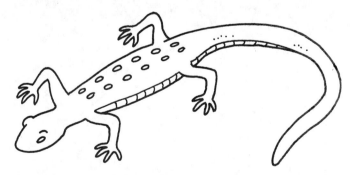

Science Sheet Notes

A Yummy Lunch, page 62—After children complete "A Yummy Lunch," have them add the following to the picture: one more plant, one more tadpole, a jelly-like cluster of eggs. **Something Sticky**, page 63—Use this sheet after children have listened to the story on page 60. This sheet is also an excellent follow-up for the activities on this page.

Name _____

A Yummy Lunch

Tadpoles live in ponds. They eat plants. Color the plants green. Color the tadpoles black. [See page 61.]

Name _____

Something Sticky

Cut out the puzzle. Put the pieces in order. Glue the pieces onto a sheet of paper. [See page 61.]

Objective: To learn that amphibians protect themselves by poison, camouflage, fleeing from enemies, and growing new body parts.

Amphibians— Watch Out!

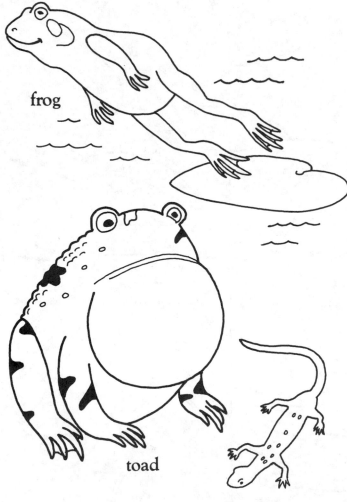

frog

toad

newt

Amphibians are small. They need to watch out for snakes, birds, and fish that want to eat them. So, many amphibians use poison from their bodies to keep enemies away. When they are in trouble, the poison oozes from under their skin. This poison can be very harmful. A toad's poison is so strong that it can even kill a bigger animal.

Some amphibians change the color of their skin to match the woods around them so they cannot be seen by their enemies. This is called *camouflage*. Did you know that in only one hour, a wood frog can change its color from dark green to light tan? When do you think a wood frog should be green? (when it hides among green leaves) ■When should it be tan? (when it hides in the brown grass and leaves)

■Some amphibians move very fast to get away from enemies. Frogs have strong back legs for jumping and hopping. Toads are not so fast, but they can frighten enemies by blowing up their bodies like huge balloons. A toad can also pull its head inside its body. What do you think it would look like then? (a rock or a much bigger, more frightening-looking animal)

■A newt has a strange way of taking care of itself. If an enemy attacks it and eats its leg, the newt can grow another one. Then it's as good as new!

Can you remember all the ways amphibians protect themselves? Name them.

Vocabulary

wart—a small hard lump that grows on the skin

☐ The Right Color!

You need: butcher paper
green, brown, and blue paint
paint brushes
copies of page 57
crayons
scissors
glue

1 Have children paint part of a large sheet of butcher paper green and brown, to represent a forest floor. Then have them paint a large area of blue in the middle of the green and brown to represent a pond.

2 Give each child a copy of page 57 and have him or her color the amphibians green and brown.

3 Help children cut out their amphibians and glue them onto the butcher paper. Place the butcher paper at a distance so children will see how the amphibians blend in with their background.

4 Ask children how they think each amphibian's color helps it protect itself from other animals. Do children know any other kinds of animals that look the same as their surroundings? [If you have already studied other classes of animals in this book, refer to them. Some mammals, birds, reptiles, and fish blend in with their surroundings too.]

☐ Let's Play Leaping Frog

Take children outdoors. Explain that a frog's long back legs make it possible for the frog to leap away from enemies. Children then pretend to be frogs and practice jumping. See how far each child can jump.

☐ Hide, Mr. Salamander

Play a game in which children sit in a circle. Make the sound of a salamander's enemy, such as the "caw-caw" of a bird or the "hiss" of a snake. When the children hear this sound, they find a place to hide. When you say, "The coast is clear. Scurry home!" the children return to the circle. If you wish, allow a child to make the sound of the enemy and then call the others back when it's safe.

☐ Can You Find Me?

You need: brown, blue, green, and gray construction paper
scissors
dark marker
tape
4 copies of page 57

1 Back a bulletin board with brown construction paper. Cut out a rounded blue shape for a pond, and add it to the bulletin board. Use a dark marker to write the words *Can You Find Me?* across the top of the board.

2 Make four copies of page 57, and cut out the amphibians.

3 Cut out four lily pads and leaves from green construction paper, and three rocks from gray construction paper. Be sure these cutouts are larger than the amphibians on page 57. Place the lily pads on the blue paper and scatter the leaves and rocks across the bulletin board on the brown paper. Be sure to attach the cutouts from the top only, so they can be lifted up.

4 Place each amphibian in its correct hiding place. [Toads under rocks, frogs on lily pads, newts and salamanders under leaves.]

5 Allow small groups to come to the bulletin board and lift up the hiding place of each amphibian.

6 At the side of your bulletin board, write the following poems about each amphibian's hiding place. If you wish, teach children the poems.

Salamander
I'm hiding, I'm hiding,
Do you know where?
Look under the leaf,
And you'll find me right there.

Toad
I'm hiding, I'm hiding,
I'm under a stone,
I'm safe and I'm snug,
In this place I call home.

Frog
I'm hiding, I'm hiding,
My color is green,
The same as the lily pad.
Can I be seen?

Science Sheet Notes

Hidden Amphibians, page 66—Remind children that amphibians must often hide to protect themselves from bigger enemies. Then give children this science sheet to complete.

How Amphibians Protect Themselves, page 67—After children complete this science sheet, have them cut apart the pictures and glue them onto a long strip of construction paper.

Name _____

Hidden Amphibians

Find the amphibians. Circle them. [See page 65.]

How many?
Circle the number.

1 2 3 4 5 6 7 8

How Amphibians Protect Themselves

Color the pictures. Trace the words. [See page 65.]

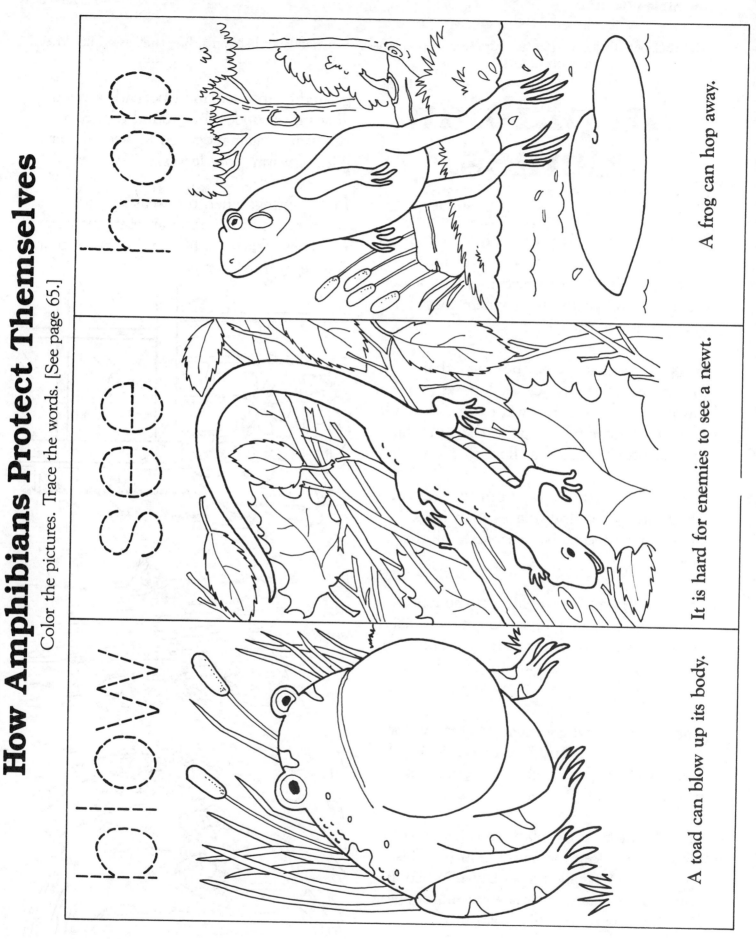

hop

A frog can hop away.

see

It is hard for enemies to see a newt.

blow

A toad can blow up its body.

Objective: To learn that as tadpoles, amphibians live in ponds and streams, but that as adults, they can live on land.

Amphibian Homes

Do you remember where baby amphibians live? ■ You will find them in quiet ponds and streams. When they grow legs for walking and lungs for breathing, they leave the water and go to places where they will stay the rest of their lives.

Frogs live in and out of the water their whole lives. They live close to ponds, so they can jump in when they want to catch food. Sometimes frogs take naps in the sun while they sit on lily pads that float in the water.

Toads travel farther away from the wet pond. They can live in drier places than frogs. They don't need to be near water all the time.

Salamanders and newts live on the forest floor in nice moist places—sometimes under leaves. If you take a summertime walk in the woods and pick up a handful of leaves, you may find a salamander.

Can you guess where mud puppies live? ■ If you said, "In the mud," you were right. Mud puppies like to live in the soft muddy earth near ponds and streams.

In wintertime, amphibians that live in cold places go to sleep for many months. This kind of sleep is called *hibernation*. When an animal hibernates, it can't even move. Before frogs hibernate, they dig holes in the

ground or into the mud beneath a pond. Toads sleep under the ground too. Some newts and salamanders go to sleep under piles of warm, cozy leaves.

In the spring, when the weather gets warmer, the hibernating amphibians wake up. They return to the pond in time to lay their eggs in the water.

68

Vocabulary

hibernate—to spend a period of time in an inactive state with a lower body temperature and metabolic rate

habitat—the area where an animal lives. Forests, jungles, oceans, deserts, polar regions, grasslands, and mountains are considered habitats.

❏ "How Many Amphibians?" Bulletin Board

Create this bulletin board to review the habitats of different amphibians.

You need: green, blue, and brown construction paper
markers
scissors
copies of page 57
oaktag
ruler

1 Back the bulletin board with green construction paper and write the title with a dark marker.

2 Cut out a large sheet of blue construction paper to represent a pond. Cut several brown shapes to represent rocks. If you wish, add more forest details.

3 Make six copies of page 57. [If you wish, enlarge the illustrations on a photocopier or with an opaque projector.] Trace and cut out the frog (six times), the toad (five times), the mud puppy (four times), and the newt (three times).

4 Make an oaktag graph as shown below. Place one of each kind of amphibian cutout on the graph. Place the other amphibian cutouts around the pond or in it.

5 Have children count the number of each kind of amphibian. Then have them color one box on the graph for each amphibian they find.

6 For younger children, omit the graph and simply ask children to count the number of each kind of amphibian. Or complete the graph as a separate activity at another time.

❏ Interview With an Amphibian

Have children pretend to be amphibians. Let them dictate adventures they have had in their woodland homes. Write their ideas on large sheets of paper and let children illustrate the stories with their own drawings, pictures from this section of the book, or photographs. Encourage children to let their imaginations soar! Here are some questions you might ask to stimulate ideas:

1 Mr. Frog, who were you playing with on the bottom of the pond ? What games did you play?

2 Miss Mud Puppy, what did you find in the slippery mud this morning? Is it something good to eat?

3 Mrs. Newt, why were you hiding under that great big leaf? Did you see something scary?

4 Little Toad, where did you get those big bumps on your back? How can you make your body grow very big right now?

Science Sheet Notes

A Home for an Amphibian, page 70—Give each child a copy of this page to complete after the children have listened to the story on page 68.

Asleep for the Winter, page 71—After children have completed their science sheets, have them add another sleeping frog, some clouds in the sky, and if they wish, snow falling to the ground.

Name _____

A Home for an Amphibian

Draw a line from each amphibian to its home. [See page 69.]

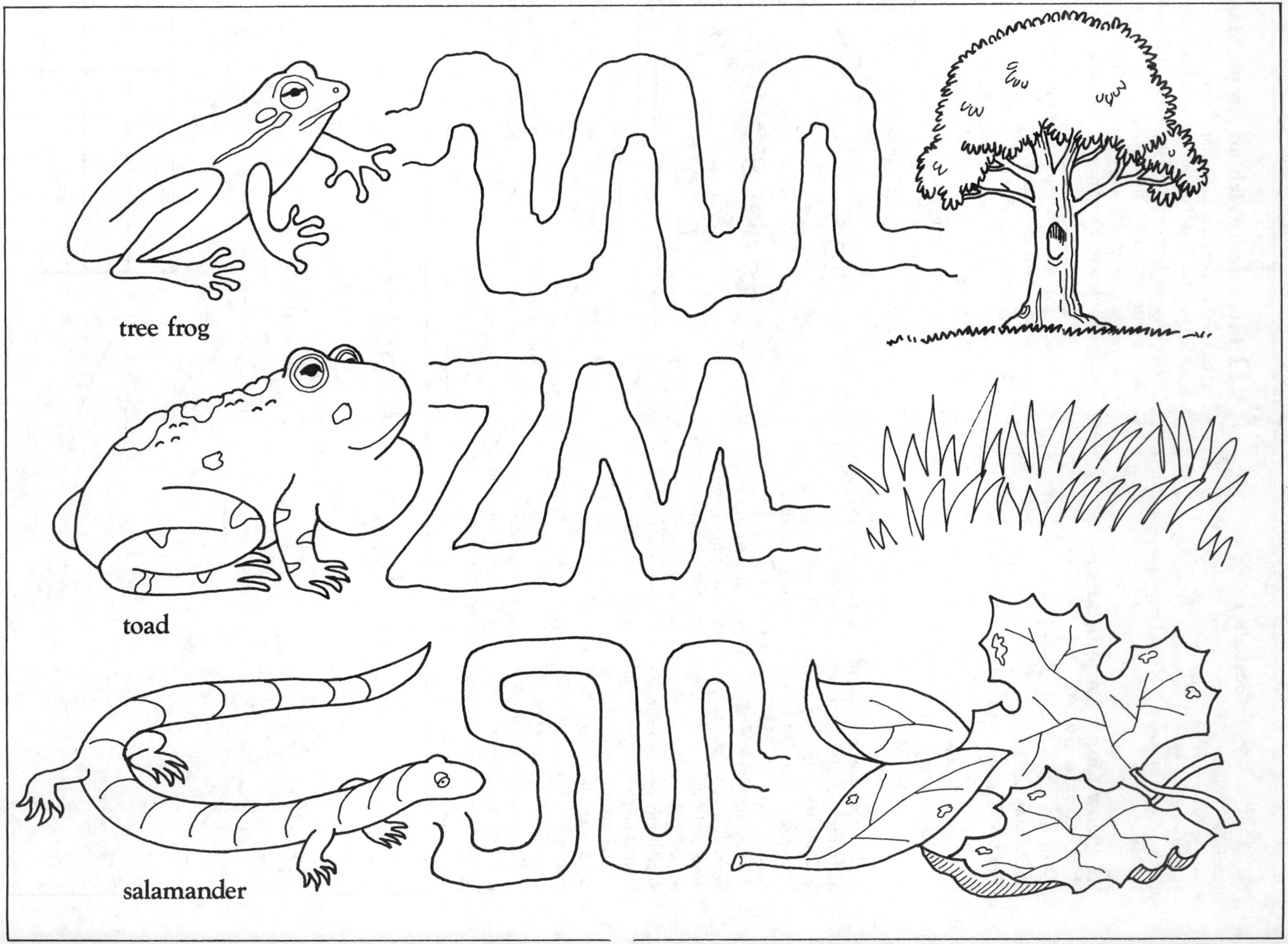

tree frog

toad

salamander

Name _____

Asleep for the Winter

Color the hibernating amphibians. Cut them out. Paste them on the picture. [See page 69.]

Objective: To learn that baby amphibians hatch from eggs, live in the water as tadpoles, and live on land as adults.

Springtime in the Pond

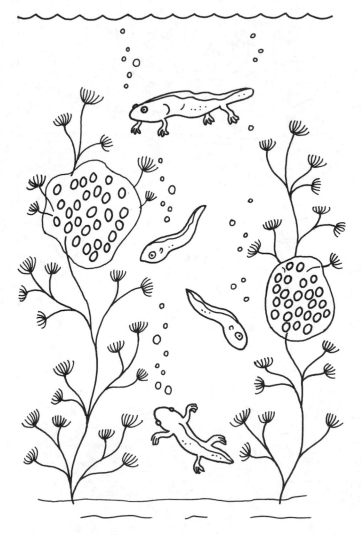

It's springtime in the pond and the amphibians have just arrived from the woods. There are frogs, toads, newts, and salamanders. Can you guess why they are here? ■ They've returned to the pond so mother amphibians can lay their jelly-covered eggs in the water. Each mother may lay hundreds, even thousands, of eggs—and when each egg hatches, a tadpole will swim out.

One mother can't take care of so many babies. Who will take care of them? [No one will.] ■ Each baby must find its own food and protect itself. That's a lot for a baby to do. When you were a baby, did you have to find your own food and take care of yourself?

Frog and toad tadpoles don't look like their parents at all. They look more like fish. They even have tails. Little by little, day by day, the tadpoles change. They start to grow legs, their tails become shorter, and soon they have lungs to help them breathe on the land. Now they are ready to leave the pond.

Some amphibians, such as frogs, like to live near ponds all their lives. Other amphibians, such as toads and salamanders, move deep into the woods. But in the spring, the amphibians return again to the pond. Now you know why. Mother amphibians need to lay eggs in the pond. Then there will soon be more baby amphibians.

hatch—to emerge from an egg

❑ A Big Newt

1 Show children the picture of the red-spotted newt on page 57 and tell them its life story: The red-spotted newt is reddish-orange in color, with dark spots on its back. It is sometimes called the red eft. Have you ever seen one? [It lives in the forests of the eastern part of the United States.] As a tadpole, the red-spotted newt lives in a pond. As an adult, it lives on the forest floor, but only for two to three years. Then it returns to lay eggs in the water. Once it is in the water, its skin color changes, forever, to brown. Its tail becomes wider, which is good for swimming. The red-spotted newt never leaves the water again. It spends the rest of its life in the pond.

2 Have children make a huge red-spotted newt to display in the classroom. Using a long sheet of butcher paper, draw an outline of the newt. [See page 57.] Have children paint it red. Draw small black eyes. Then cut it out and have children paint black spots on the newt's back.

If you prefer, try this activity with the Western newt, which lives along the Pacific coast. It is twice the size of the red-spotted newt and is dark brown in color with a yellow or orange underbelly. Adult Western newts return to the water to lay their eggs, but they go back to the woods afterwards. They do not change color. Have children paint the butcher paper dark brown. Cut it out and let children paint the newt's belly yellow or orange.

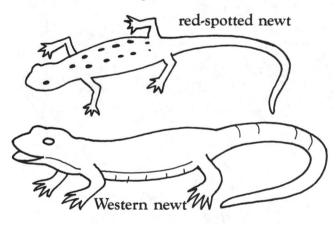

red-spotted newt

Western newt

❑ Observing Frogs' Eggs

1 If you have access to a pond where frogs are breeding in the spring, scoop up a few dozen frog eggs. Keep the eggs in pond water in your class aquarium, and add a few water plants. Make sure your aquarium gets some sunlight during the day. Place a hand lens near the aquarium so children can see the eggs close up. Let them make drawings of the eggs. Children will discover that each egg is enclosed in a jelly-like capsule. They can watch the eggs daily as the eggs develop into tadpoles. This can take from three to twenty-one days. Record children's observations on a chart and add their drawings.

2 If you don't have access to a breeding pond, you can purchase frog eggs from Insect Lore Products, P.O. Box 1535, Shafter, CA 93263. [You get 6-10 grass frog eggs in each package.] Your class can watch the growth from eggs into tadpoles and then into adult frogs. Allow 2-4 weeks for delivery.

❑ Eggs in Jelly?

Have children touch peppercorns in a bowl of egg whites. The sensation is pretty similar to frogs' eggs in their jelly-like case.

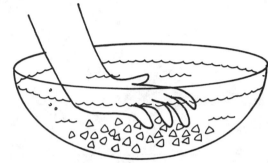

❑ Amphibian Jigsaws

Children love puzzles. Amphibian Life-Cycle Jigsaw Puzzles are available from Insect Lore [See address in Observing Frogs' Eggs.]

Science Sheet Notes

How Toads Grow, page 74—Have children write a number from 1 to 3 in each circle to show how a toad grows. Then have children color the pictures, cut them out, and paste them in order on a long strip of paper.

Back to the Pond, page 75—Remind children that newts live on land as adults, but return to the pond to lay eggs in the spring. Then give them this science sheet to complete.

Name _____

How Toads Grow

Color the pictures. Cut them out. Paste them in order on a long strip of paper. [See page 73.]

Name _____

Back to the Pond

Color the newt red. Trace a path through the maze to the pond. Circle each amphibian you pass. [See page 73.]

Objective: To learn about a frog's characteristics.

Frogs

Lots of people like frogs. They are good jumpers and they're fun to watch. Some children even keep frogs as pets. Do you have one?

■ Most frogs are very small. The Western tree frog is so small, it can sit on top of one of your fingers. But some frogs are very big. Did you know that the giant frog of West Africa is as big as a small dog?

■ Most frogs live on the ground near ponds or streams, but some frogs live in bushes and in treetops. These frogs have little suckers on the ends of their feet to help them hold onto branches.

Frogs are good jumpers and swimmers because they have long back legs with toes that are webbed. Have you ever seen webbed toes? ■ Webbed toes look like swimming fins. Did you ever swim with fins on your feet? ■ Fins help you swim very fast, like a frog!

Frogs like to eat insects, spiders, earthworms, and tiny fish. How do you think they catch these animals? [A frog has a long, sticky tongue that it can quickly flip out to capture food.]

■ Most frogs have green or brown skin, but some frogs are covered with spots. The leopard frog has green and brown spots that remind some people of the spots on a leopard. Did you know that frogs shed their skin as they grow? ■ When their bodies get too big for their skin, their old skin peels off, and a new skin takes its place. Have you ever found a frog's old skin in the woods? ■ It is very thin and light.

During the winter you won't see frogs in cold places. Can you guess why not? ■ Frogs go to sleep, or hibernate, down in the mud under lakes and ponds. They don't wake up until the spring. Then you can find lots of them back in the ponds.

leopard frog

tree frog

Frog

webbed feet—feet that have skin between the toes
sucker—an organ in various animals used for adhering or holding onto things

❏ "A Frog Has..." Bulletin Board

You need: light-colored and blue construction paper
colored markers
copies of page 80
oaktag
pencil
scissors

1 Back the bulletin board with light-colored construction paper.
2 With a dark marker, write the title, *A Frog Has...* at the top of the bulletin board.
3 Use an opaque projector to enlarge the frog on a lily pad from page 80, and trace it onto oaktag. [If you prefer, trace the frog and lily pad directly without enlarging it.]
4 Color the frog green, but do not color the lily pad. Cut out the frog and lily pad and place them on a large sheet of blue construction paper to represent the pond. If desired, cut out small, simple fish-shapes and place them in the pond.
5 On a sheet of oaktag, write the information shown on the illustration below. Do not fill in the numerals. [For younger children, draw small pictures of the words instead of writing them.]
6 Have children come to the bulletin board and count the frog's characteristics with you. Fill in the missing numbers. [Older children might enjoy the challenge of finding the number of characteristics of two or three frogs.]

❏ Did You Know?

People often confuse frogs with toads. Discuss the differences and create an experience chart. Add lots of pictures and children's drawings. Here are some ideas.

Frogs

Frogs are green or brown.
Frogs have smooth, wet skin.
Frogs live in ponds and on land.
Frogs run away from enemies.
Frogs have long hind legs.

Toads

Toads are darker than frogs.
Toads have bumpy, dry skin.
Toads live on the land.
Toads can blow up their bodies to scare enemies.
Toads have shorter legs than frogs.

❏ The Frog Song

Teach children this delightful song about frogs. When they are familiar with the words, have them squat in a large circle and pretend to be frogs. Whenever they sing the word "Brrr---ump!" they jump up.

Lis - ten to the song of the
Frogs in yon - der pond:
Crick, crick, crick - e - ty crick,
Brrr - - - - ump!

❏ Frog and Toad

Read aloud some of Arnold Lobel's *Frog and Toad* books: *Frog and Toad*, *Frog and Toad Are Friends*, and *Frog and Toad Together* (Harper and Row). Then ask children some of these questions:
1 Do you think frogs and toads can really do the things they do in these stories? [No.]
2 Can frogs and toads really talk the way people do? [No.]
3 What sound can frogs and toads make? [Most male frogs and toads can croak. They inflate a sac in their throat to make this sound. Have children try croaking!]
4 Can frogs and toads really walk on two legs the way the characters do in the stories? [No. Frogs and toads don't walk at all. They jump, hop, and swim, and they need all four legs to help them.]
5 Can frogs and toads really read and write? [No.]
6 What *can* they do that people do? [They can grow, breathe in and out, eat, have babies, and protect themselves from enemies.]

❏ Your Own "Frog and Toad"

After reading Arnold Lobel's tales, have children think up their own adventures of Frog and Toad. They can dictate their stories to you or record them on tape.

Science Sheet Notes

Who Am I?, page 79—This science sheet can be completed before you read the story on page 76 or as a culminating activity for this section of the book.
Frog on the Pond, page 80—Have children color the frog green and cut it out along the solid lines. Fold it on the dotted lines. Then cut out the lily pad. Trace it onto a piece of styrofoam and cut it out again. Attach the frog to the lily pad and float them in a large bowl of water.

Who Am I?

Connect the dots from 1 to 20. Color the picture. Answer the question. [See page 78.]

At first I live in a pond.
I look like a little fish.
Then I live on land.
I have smooth green skin.
I am good at jumping.

Who am I? _____

Frog on the Pond

[Instructions on page 78.]

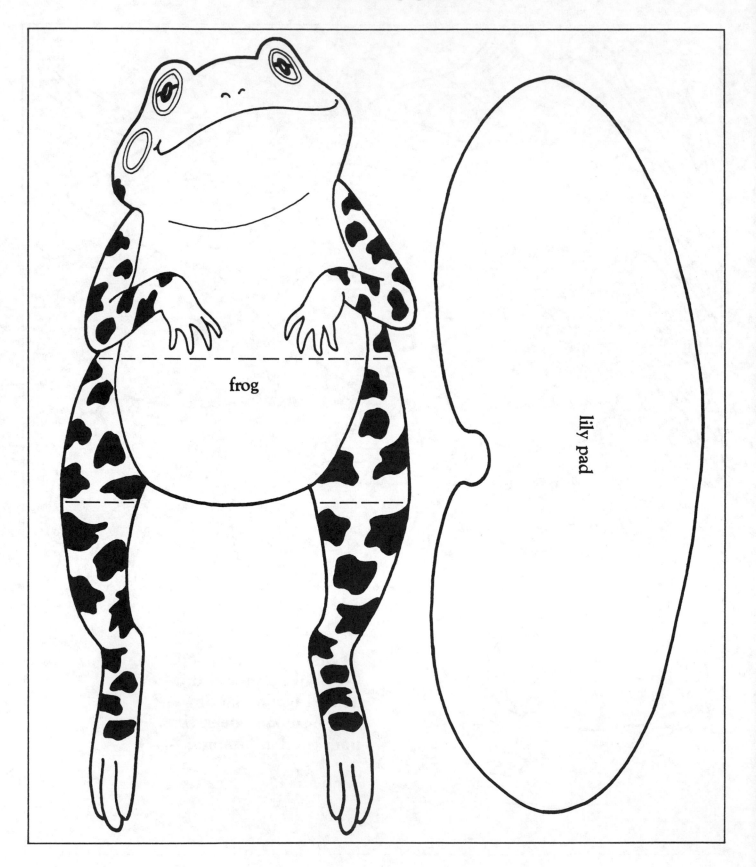

frog

lily pad

Reptiles

Our Reptile Center

turtle

alligator

snake

lizard

Where do reptiles hibernate?

When the weather turns cold, reptiles hibernate. Snakes and lizards go into holes or crawl under rocks. Turtles dig into the mud under a pond. Tortoises dig holes under rotten leaves.

This is Felix. He is a lizard. He eats insects. Felix is a REPTILE.

My Favorite Reptile

lizard · snake · turtle · alligator

Objective: To learn about three groups of reptiles—(1) *lizards and snakes*, (2) *turtles*, and (3) *crocodiles and alligators*.

Clunk, Clunk, Clunk

The ground shook when he walked. He was very heavy and taller than a tree. Some people would say he looked like a dragon. He was an animal that you can't find on earth anymore. Can you guess what he was?

■Right, he was a dinosaur! Scientists believe dinosaurs belonged to a group of animals called reptiles. Although there are no more dinosaurs, we still have lots of reptiles in our world. Lizards and snakes! Turtles! And crocodiles and alligators! They're all reptiles! Have you ever seen any of these animals?

■No matter where you live, you can probably find lizards and snakes. But sometimes they're hard to see. They try to hide from people because they are shy and easily frightened.

A lizard has four legs, a long tail, and eyelids. Count your legs: 1, 2! Now blink your eyes and touch your eyelids! Now tell me this: How many legs does a snake have? ■A snake doesn't have legs! You'll never catch a snake blinking his eyes either, because he doesn't have eyelids! So how can he close his eyes to sleep? [Snakes sleep with their eyes open.]

■Turtles have something that no other reptiles have, and they carry them on their backs. Guess! (a shell) ■They pull their heads, legs, and tails into their shells whenever they want to hide.

Now you've probably heard about crocodiles in the story of *Peter Pan*. Crocodiles, and their cousins the alligators, have powerful tails and strong jaws with sharp teeth. They always live in or near water. They have webbed feet, which means they have skin between their toes, to help them swim. Have you ever seen people use flippers on their feet to help them swim?

■All reptiles—lizards and snakes, turtles, and crocodiles and alligators—have dry scaly skin. They never sweat so they don't lose water through their skins. Many reptiles can go for months without a drink. How long do you think you could go without drinking?

dinosaur

The Reptiles

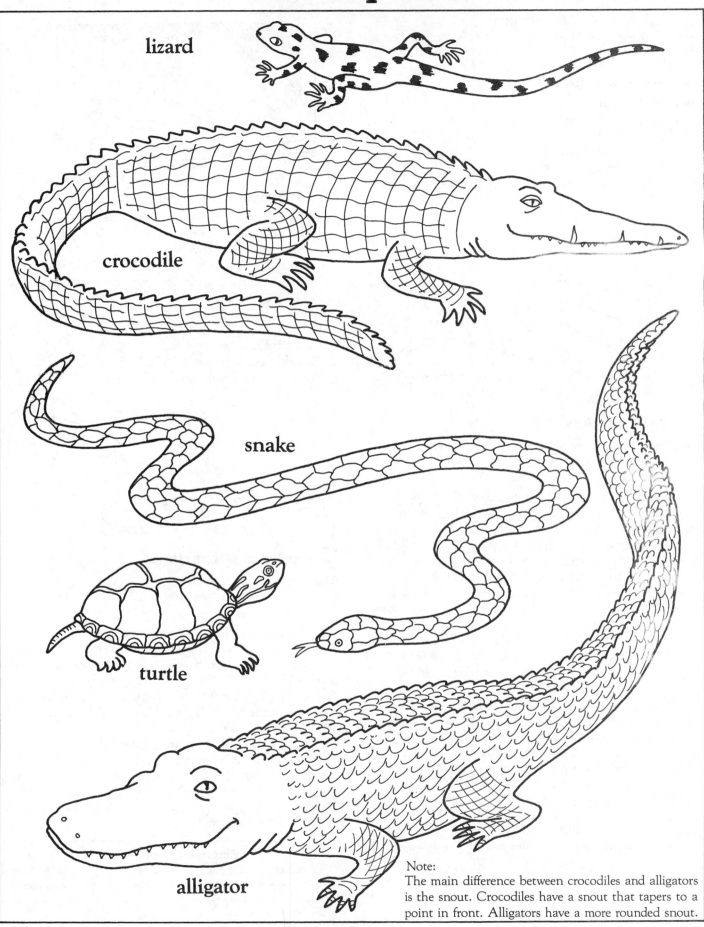

lizard

crocodile

snake

turtle

alligator

Note:
The main difference between crocodiles and alligators is the snout. Crocodiles have a snout that tapers to a point in front. Alligators have a more rounded snout.

83

Vocabulary

molting—When an animal begins to shed its skin because a new skin is growing under the old, we say that the animal is molting.

☐ Snake Dough Recipe

You need: 4 cups flour

        ¹/₂ cup salt

        1¹/₂ cups water

        1 tablespoon oil

        green food coloring

Mix all ingredients together. Knead until dough is smooth. Give a half-cup ball of dough to each child.

☐ Make Snakes!

You need: clay or modeling dough (recipe above)

        construction paper

        sequins

Give each child a chunk of clay or dough. Show the youngsters how to roll their chunks into snakes. As they work, share these facts:

☐ A forked tongue helps the snake gather smells and track animals. [Make forked tongues from construction paper. Have each child add a tongue to his or her snake.]

☐ A snake's eyes are always open. They are covered with clear scales to keep them from drying out. [Have children use sequins to make eyes.]

☐ Snakes cannot live where the ground stays frozen all year. [Because snakes are cold-blooded, they cannot move about in freezing weather. If the weather is always cold, the snake cannot hunt prey.]

☐ The smallest snake—the Braminy blind snake of the tropics—is only 6″ long.

☐ The South American anaconda is one of the longest snakes. It can grow to more than 37′!

☐ Some snakes in zoos have been able to go without eating for as long as three years.

☐ Some snakes *molt* or shed their skins as often as six times a year.

☐ The Ringhals is a kind of African cobra that can squirt poison into the eyes of a victim that is 6′ to 8′ away.

☐ Lizardterium

Lizards are among the easiest reptiles to keep in the classroom. For a lizard home, you need a glass aquarium and aluminum or copper screen to put on top. Lizards are available at most pet shops. They need very little water. Follow pet shop recommendations for feeding and decorating the interior of the aquarium.

Once you have the lizard in its home, ask the children:

☐ How many legs does our lizard have?

☐ Does our lizard have eyelids?

☐ How does our lizard's skin look?

☐ What should we name our lizard?

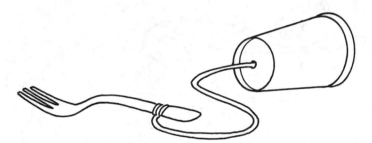

☐ Feel the Vibrations

You need: string

        metal fork or spoon

        paper cup

1 Ask children what they think it would be like if they could *not* hear. Explain that snakes do not hear well. They don't have ears on their heads as we do. But snakes are very good at feeling vibrations. All sound makes vibrations.

2 Have children rest their heads against a wooden table top (ears against the table). Tap a fork against the table. Ask children if they can *feel* the sound.

3 Tie one end of the string around the fork or spoon. Punch a hole in the bottom of the cup, pull the other end of the string through the cup, and knot the string so that it will stay in the cup. Have each child, in turn, put the cup over his or her ear as you tap the dangling fork. Can children feel as well as hear the vibrations?

Science Sheet Notes

Reptile Hunt, page 85—After reading the story on page 82, use this science sheet to help children learn to recognize reptiles.

Reptile Hunt

Circle the snake, alligator, crocodile, lizard, and turtles. Color the picture. [See page 84.]

Objective: To learn that reptiles primarily eat other animals (although some lizards and turtles are plant eaters).

Rattles

It was a hot summer day and a big fat snake, named Rattles, had just awakened from a long afternoon nap in the shade. He was hungry! He hadn't eaten for a week. All the animals who saw him wake up started hiding. They knew he'd eat the first thing that came along.

Reptiles, after all, aren't very picky about food. They eat just about anything they can swallow! Snakes, like old Rattles, prefer to eat animals. Rattles is probably looking for a mouse or rabbit right now! He's one of those lucky snakes that has poison to help catch his meals. He simply bites the animal he wants to eat with his poison fangs, and the animal stops struggling as the poison goes to work. When it's still, Rattles swallows it.

Of course, some snakes don't use poison—because they don't have any. Boa constrictors are snakes that wrap themselves around what they want to eat and squeeze. Pretty soon, the animal that's getting squeezed stops moving because it can't breathe … and down the snake's mouth it goes!

Crocodiles and alligators are reptiles that also like to eat other animals. They catch them in their powerful jaws and then hold them underwater till they stop struggling. Then what do you think they do? [They swallow them!]

■ Turtles and lizards are reptiles that usually eat only plants, insects, and spiders. Lizards have long sticky tongues that help them catch about any insect that flies too close!

Most reptiles can go for a long time between meals. Some snakes may only eat four big meals a year. How would you feel if you had to wait three months between meals?

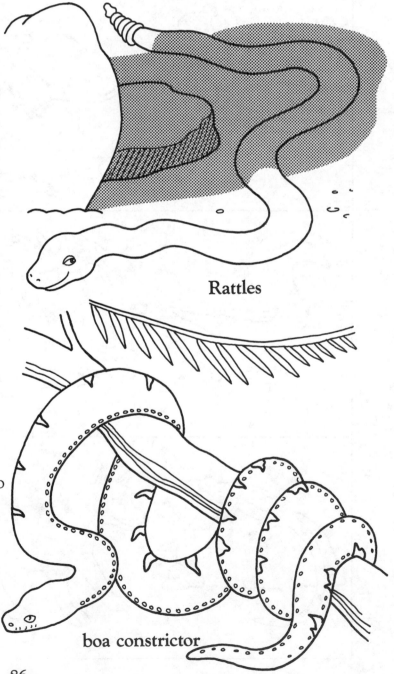

Rattles

boa constrictor

☐ Land/Water Bulletin Board

You need: blue and brown construction paper
black marker
magazines and paste

1 Copy the pictures on this page for each child. Ask children to color and cut out the pictures.
2 Prepare the board by covering half of it with blue paper and half with brown paper. Create a border around the board with the reptiles the children have colored. At the top of the blue paper write, "Water Reptiles Eat ..." At the top of the brown paper write, "Land Reptiles Eat ..."
3 Help children find magazine pictures of animals that reptiles living in water might eat (fish, frogs, water insects). Let them paste their pictures on the blue side of the board. Repeat the activity for land reptiles (which eat small mammals, birds, and insects).
4 Follow up the activity with a discussion of how reptiles help people. [They eat insect and rodent pests that destroy food crops, such as corn.] Also discuss how each kind of reptile has adapted itself to hunting for food in its environment. [Sea turtles are wonderful swimmers, with powerful front legs that work like flippers. Lizards have tongues that are sticky—for catching flying insects.]

☐ Snake Trick Experiment

You need: a long balloon (uninflated)
a small block, a little larger than the mouth of the balloon

1 Explain that snakes can swallow things that are wider than their mouths. They don't have to chew their food, so they just swallow it whole. Ask if anyone thinks he or she could swallow a whole hamburger without chewing.
2 Show children how a snake's mouth and body stretch when it eats. Tell children to pretend that the balloon is a snake and the block is a whole piece of food. [What food might the snake eat?] Place the balloon on the table. Stretch the mouth of the balloon wide enough so the block goes inside. Work the block down into the balloon. Let each child try this demonstration.
3 If possible, take children to a zoo at snake-feeding time.

Science Sheet Notes

Lizard Lunch, page 88—After children have listened to the story on page 86, use this science sheet. Remind children that most lizards eat insects and spiders.
Alligator River Maze, page 89—Explain that the alligator on this page is going to the beach to sunbathe. Remind children that alligators will eat almost any animal they can catch.

☐ Missing Monkeys Finger Play

Teach children this finger play and remind them that alligators and crocodiles are dangerous.

Five little monkeys, sitting in a tree.	[Hold up fingers on one hand.]
Said to each other, "Gator can't catch me!"	[Wiggle fingers on one hand.]
Along comes the gator, quiet as can be,	[Other hand moves toward wiggling fingers.]
And SNAP! There's one less monkey in the tree.	[Gator hand grabs one finger on monkey hand and folds it down.]

Continue with "Four little monkeys, sitting in a tree," etc.

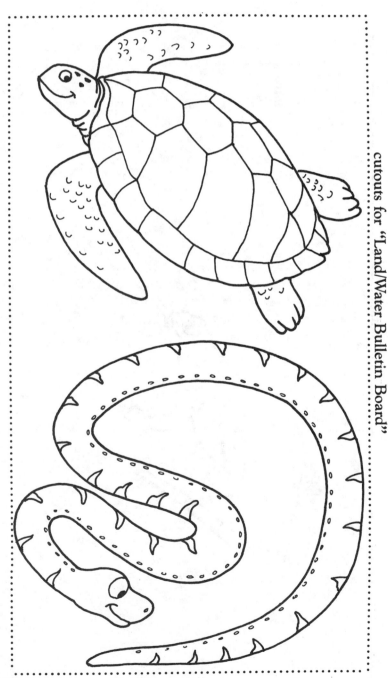

cutouts for "Land/Water Bulletin Board"

Lizard Lunch

Draw lines from the lizard's tongue to the animals it might eat. Color the lizard.
[See page 87.]

Alligator River Maze

Name _____

Draw a line inside the river from the alligator to the beach. As you pass animals that the alligator might eat, circle them. Color the picture. [See page 87.]

START

BEACH

FINISH

89

Objective: To learn that reptiles use bluffing, camouflage, escape, and fighting to protect themselves from enemies.

The Tricksters!

Reptiles play lots of tricks on animals that want to eat them. There's a lizard in Australia that uses a really good trick to frighten enemies. He stands up on his hind legs to look tall, fills his body with air to look big, and then hisses really loudly! If you bumped into someone who could do this, would you be afraid?

■ Most lizards have another good trick. Whenever an animal tries to catch a lizard by grabbing onto its long tail, the tail breaks off and the lizard runs away! If a lizard could talk, he'd probably say, "You keep the tail, darlin', I can always grow another one!"

Some African lizards can change the colors of their skins to blend in with the colors around them. Remember what that's called? (camouflage) ■ The most famous color changer is the chameleon.

Snakes can't change their colors, but many of them are the color of the ground they crawl over. Many animals are careful around snakes because they think they are poisonous—and some are! The rattlesnake is a poisonous snake that makes a sound to warn enemies away. Guess what sound!

■ Now snakes have another way of protecting themselves. Because they're long and thin, they can slip into places other animals can't fit. Pigs love to eat snakes ... but how can a pig fit inside a snake's hole?

■ Turtles have an easy way of protecting themselves. Guess! [They pull their heads and legs inside their hard shells. Enemies can't crack the shells.] ■ Some turtles also can make a bad smell to frighten enemies away. Name another animal that uses smell to get rid of enemies. (skunk)

■ Crocodiles and alligators have mouths full of teeth and powerful tails. Do you think they hide from other animals? ■ No way— they aren't afraid to fight anyone.

There's one time in each reptile's life when it has almost no protection from enemies. That's just after it's born. Can you guess why? [Babies are smaller and weaker than adult animals.]

❑ Hidden Reptiles Hide-and-Seek

You need: copies of page 92
              paste
              construction paper

1 Copy page 92 five times. Paste each copy on a sheet of construction paper or oaktag. [If desired, laminate the pages for durability.] Cut apart the cards. Hide four sets of the cards around the room before children arrive.
2 Before the game, explain to children that all reptiles would rather hide from enemies than fight them. In fact, the only way that some reptiles have of defending themselves is by hiding.
3 Post the set of cards you have not hidden. Tell children that you've hidden pictures of reptiles around the room. When you give the signal, everyone starts looking for the cards. The first child to find one of each card is the winner. Children who find several cards of the same kind but lack one of the other three may trade their extras with other children. [Note: You may also divide the class into teams of 4-5 children, and let one team at a time look for cards.]

❑ Reptile Checklist

✔Have children pantomime: a turtle going into its shell, a rattlesnake rattling, an alligator crawling.
✔Read Aesop's Fable *The Tortoise and the Hare*.
✔Make a bar graph of children's favorite reptiles.
✔Have children make snake chains by pasting strips of paper into circles that interlock.
✔Order an American chameleon from Carolina Biological Supply Company (2700 York Road; Burlington, NC 27215-3398; Phone 1-800-334-5551).

❑ Walnut Shell Turtle

Give each child a copy of this turtle to paste onto construction paper and cut out. Have children color their turtles. Then give each of them half of a walnut shell. Show them how to paste the shell to their turtles' backs. Hold turtle races!

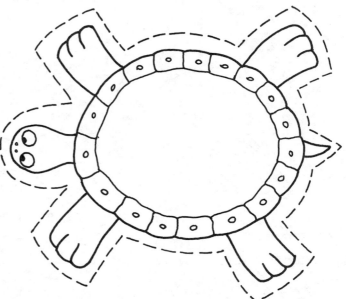

❑ Turtle Poem

Teach the children this poem:

A turtle is a reptile, its home is on its back.
It never has to worry if someone will attack.
When it spies an enemy, what does it do so well?
It simply takes its head and feet and pops inside its shell.

Now write your own poems with the children!

Science Sheet Notes

Hidden Reptiles, page 92—Use the cards as explained in the Hidden Reptiles Hide-and-Seek game. Extend the activity by having children color the cards and staple them together to make "Reptile Defenses" minibooks.
Build a Turtle, page 93—Have each child paste this sheet onto construction paper and color all the parts before cutting out the turtle pieces. Help children attach the legs and head to the shell with brass fasteners.

Hidden Reptiles

Use these cards with the game on page 91.

Name _____

Build A Turtle

Cut along the heavy lines. Put together the parts with brass fasteners. [See page 91.]

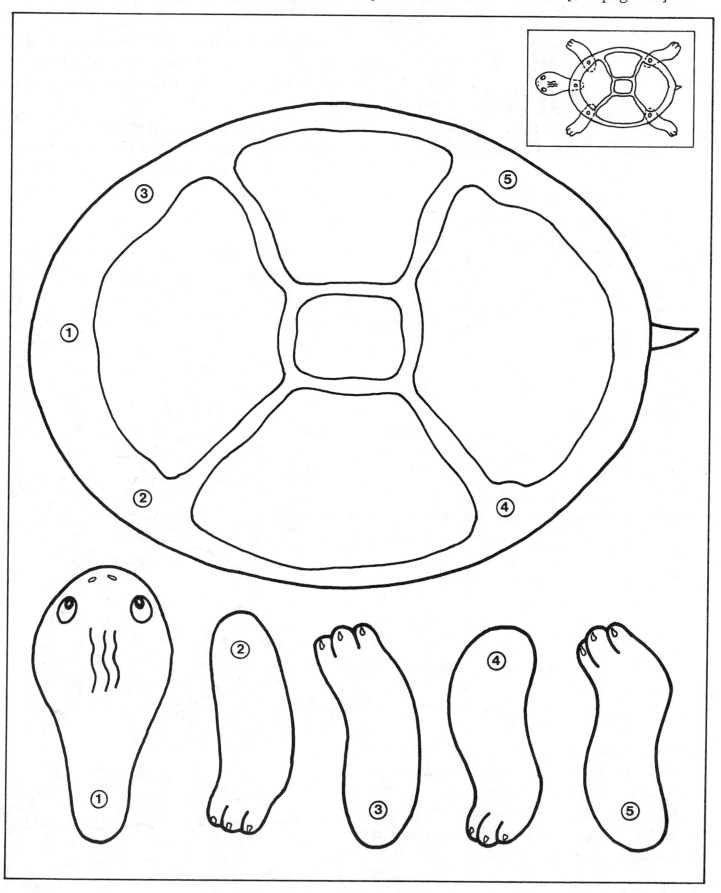

Objective: To learn that reptiles prefer warm climates and hibernate during cold periods in cooler climates.

We Like Sunshine

I have a friend named Suzie who has a turtle. She got him at the pet store. "But where did he live," I wondered, "before that?"

I went to the pet store and asked Sam, the man who owns it, where turtles come from. This is what he told me.

"Turtles live almost everywhere in the world. Most of them live in lakes or rivers or in the oceans. Suzie's turtle came from a lake in Mexico. Turtles that live on land are called tortoises instead of turtles."

Sam said that most reptiles like warm weather. For example, alligators and crocodiles only live in places that are hot. They love sunshine and they love water! In the mornings, they like to lie on the banks of rivers and sunbathe. When they get too hot, they slip into the cool water and float. Only their eyes are above the water's surface. That way they can watch. What do you think they're watching for? (animals to eat)

■ Sam told me that lizards and snakes also like to live where it's warm, but that plenty of lizards and snakes live in places that have wintertime. When the weather turns real cold, the snakes and lizards hibernate. That means that they go into a deep sleep until

the weather warms up. When they're ready to sleep, they usually go into a hole in the ground or a cave or they crawl under a rock.

Sam said that turtles and tortoises also hibernate. Tortoises dig a hole under rotten leaves and plants, and turtles dig into the mud at the bottom of the ponds, lakes, or streams that they live in.

Now I've decided that I want a pet reptile—either a lizard or a turtle. Which one would you choose?

turtle

tortoise

alligator

94

Vocabulary

hibernate—to sleep through cold spells
burrow—to dig underground; a place where a hibernating animal stays
cold-blooded—When an animal's body temperature changes with the temperature of its environment, the animal is cold-blooded.

❏ Hot and Cold Reptiles

You need:　heavy aluminum foil
　　　　　　　scissors

1 Explain that reptiles are cold-blooded. That means that the animal's body temperature is about the same as the ground it is on or the water it is in. Also explain that reptiles must be warm in order to move quickly.
2 Cut a lizard or snake shape out of heavy aluminum foil. Place it outside in the sun. After a few minutes, have children feel it. How does it feel?
　Next, put the foil cutout in the freezer or in ice water for a few minutes. Take it out. Let the children feel it.
3 Explain that real reptiles get hot on hot days almost as quickly as did the cutout reptile when placed in the sun, and they get cold on cold days almost as quickly as did the cutout when placed in the freezer or water. That's because the blood in their bodies doesn't stay warm all the time like people's blood.

❏ Where to Sleep

1 Hibernation. Explain that reptiles try to find places to hibernate where they will not be disturbed as they sleep. Some of them dig holes or burrows in the ground, some of them find rocks to crawl under, some of them burrow or dig under the mud at the bottom of ponds or streams. As hibernation begins, the animal falls into a deep sleep. It breathes less often than normal and its heart beats much slower than normal—which means that less food energy is used than when the animal is awake. The sleeping reptile won't wake up until the ground or water around it warms up.
2 Winter walk. When the weather turns cold, take the children into a wooded area. Ask them to try to spot places that would make good hibernation places. Encourage them not to disturb any sleepers that they find. Talk about why each spot identified is or is not a good hibernation place.

❏ Hibernate—After Lunch!

After children have eaten lunch or snacks, explain that reptiles eat lots of food before they hibernate. The food helps keep them alive while they sleep. One of the reasons that they hibernate is because their food supplies become low in winter. What do reptiles eat? (plants and animals that become harder to find in cold weather)
　Have children pretend to be reptiles that are ready to hibernate. They've just eaten to fatten themselves up for the long winter sleep. Ask each child to tell what kind of reptile he or she is and then find a good place to hibernate in. Remind children that hibernators need a safe, hidden place to sleep. Provide boxes, blankets, etc., to create the hibernation chambers. [This is a good activity to use an an entree into naptime!]

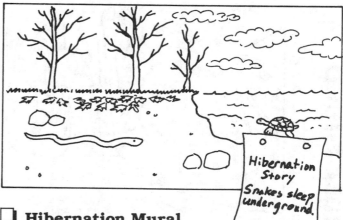

❏ Hibernation Mural

You need:　butcher paper (or other mural paper)
　　　　　　　marker
　　　　　　　blue and brown paint
　　　　　　　brushes
　　　　　　　paper
　　　　　　　animal stencils or pictures

1 Draw a line across the center of the paper as shown. Have children paint the space above the line blue (for sky) and the space below the line brown (for earth). Have them add trees and lakes to the scene, as desired.
2 Have children use stencils to trace reptile shapes onto paper. Let them color and cut out the shapes and place them on the mural. [They may also use reptile pictures cut from magazines.]
3 Write a hibernation story with the children and place it next to the mural.

Science Sheet Notes

Winter Sleep, page 96—Give children this sheet to complete after they have participated in any of the hibernation activities on this page.
At Home in Water, page 97—Explain to children that some reptiles must live close to water: turtles, certain snakes, and alligators and crocodiles. Then give them this sheet. Tell them to circle only the animals that are reptiles.

Name _____

Winter Sleep

Circle the 5 hibernating reptiles in this picture. Color the picture. [See page 95.]

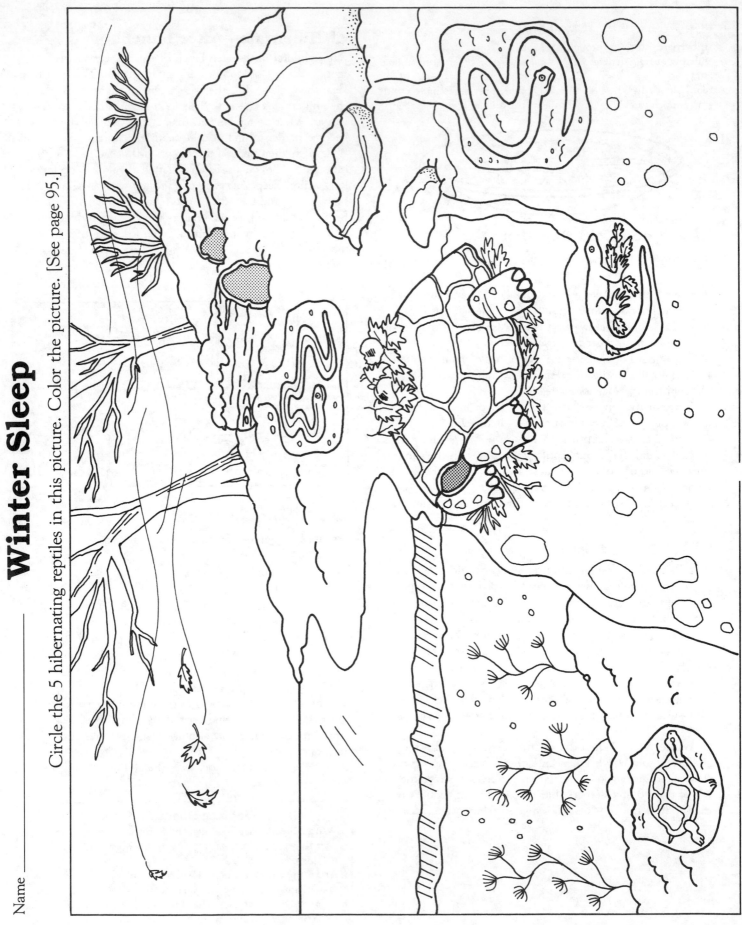

96

Name _____

At Home in Water

All of the animals in this picture live near water. Circle only the reptiles. Color the picture. [See page 95.]

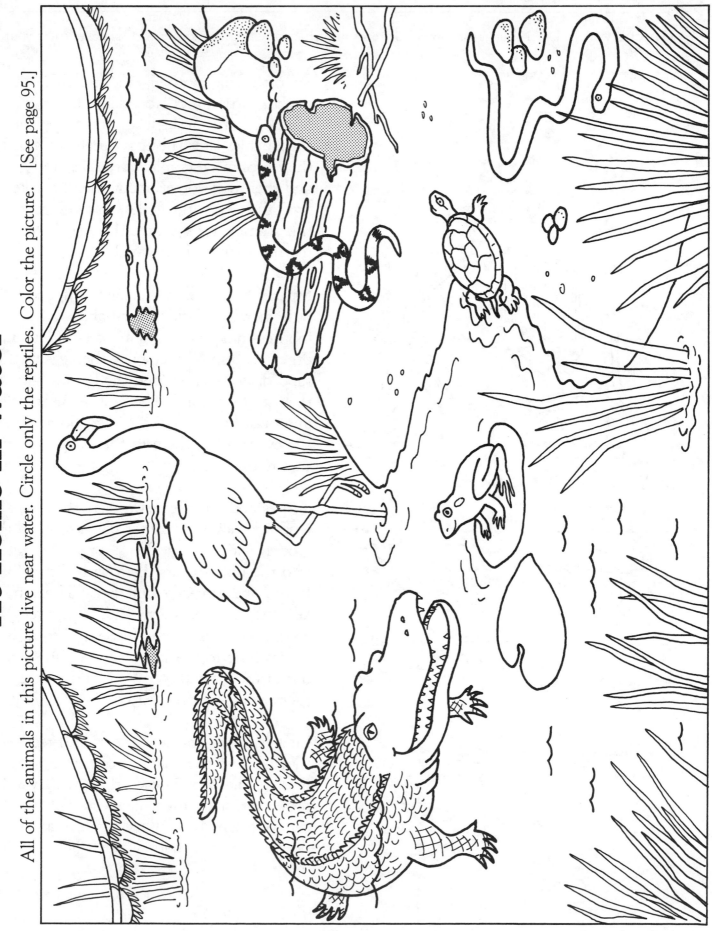

97

Objective: To learn that most reptiles lay eggs and that most reptile mothers do not rear their young.

No Time for Kids

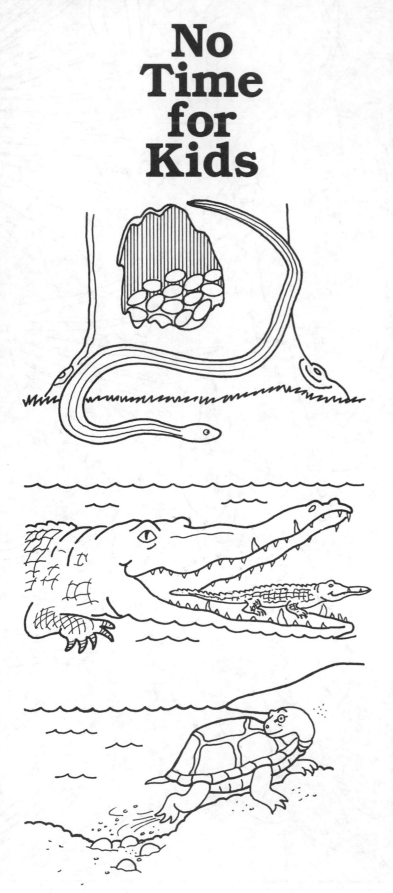

Most reptile mothers—mother snakes, lizards, turtles, and crocodiles—lay eggs. Mother lizards and snakes don't stay with their babies after the eggs hatch. Lizards lay their eggs in nests made of leaves and grass and then they forget about them. Snakes drop their eggs into holes, rotten logs, or tree stumps. By the time the eggs hatch, mother snake is long gone!

Mother crocodiles and alligators spend a little more time with their babies. The mothers hide their eggs in nests of leaves and other rubbish or they bury the eggs in the sand on a beach. When the babies hatch, they start grunting. The mother hears them and digs them out of the nest. Sometimes she even carries them to the water. Then they're on their own.

Turtles and tortoises always lay their eggs on land. Usually the mother digs a hole in the ground with her back legs, drops the eggs into the hole, covers them with dirt or leaves, and forgets about them. The sun keeps the ground warm and, after a few weeks, the eggs hatch. Turtle and tortoise babies have to break out of their shells, dig out of the ground, get food, and protect themselves—all on their own!

Luckily, reptile babies have special teeth that they can use to break out of the eggs. And most reptile babies—even though they're in some danger from enemies—are able to take care of themselves. What would happen if a newborn human baby was left alone by its mother?

❏ Reptile Egg Hunt

You need: small (plastic) foil-wrapped eggs

1 Before beginning this activity, hide 20-30 eggs in a small area outside. [If you prefer, eggs may be hidden inside the classroom.] Choose hiding places typical of reptiles—under leaves, in tree stumps, etc.

2 When class begins, talk about eggs with the children. Ask them why they think eggs have shells. (to keep the baby safe from the outside; to keep the baby and its food, which is inside the shell, from drying out) What do they think is inside the shell? (the baby reptile; food for the baby) How long does the baby have to stay in the shell? (until it is grown-up enough to care for itself outside of the shell: "caring for itself" means finding food and defending against enemies)

3 Then ask children how they think reptiles keep their eggs safe from other animals. Remind them that most reptiles don't stay with their eggs after laying them (unlike birds). [Most reptiles try to lay eggs out of sight of predators. Many reptiles, however, are careless about hiding eggs; consequently, many reptile eggs are stolen by predators.]

4 Tell children that you have hidden "pretend" reptile eggs outside. Take them outside and let the hunt begin!

❏ To the Zoo

If you are near a zoo, find out if it has a reptile collection. If it does, ask if the zoo is incubating reptile eggs or if one of the reptiles has recently laid eggs. If so, arrange a field trip to view the eggs with the children.

❏ Lights Out Turtle Crawl

1 Explain that when baby turtles break out of their shells and dig their way out of the sand, they crawl as quickly as they can for water. The longer it takes them to get to the sea, the more danger they are in from birds and other reptiles that want to eat them. The babies usually wait until it is almost nighttime to crawl across the beach to the sea—that's when it's hardest for enemies to see them.

2 Clear a space in the room. Have 4-5 children line up on one end of the space and get down on hands and knees. Tell them they are baby turtles that have just hatched. They are waiting for it to get dark so they can race to the sea (at the other end of the cleared space). When you flip off the lights, all the baby turtles crawl for the sea. When you flip the lights back on, all the turtles freeze. Continue flipping the lights on and off until one child reaches the sea. He or she is the winner. Repeat activity with other groups of children for as long as there is interest.

Science Sheet Notes

Turtle Birth, page 100—After children have played "Lights Out Turtle Crawl" above, give each child a copy of this sheet. Explain that the pictures tell the story of how baby turtles are born. Give each child a $4^1/_2$″ × 20″ strip of construction paper to paste their pictures on.

Find the Babies, page 101—Tell children that most reptile babies look like their parents. Then have them complete this sheet.

Turtle Birth

Name _____

Color the pictures. Cut them out along the dotted lines. Put them in order on a long strip of construction paper. [See page 99.]

1. Mother turtle digs a hole.

2. She drops her eggs in the hole.

3. She covers the eggs with soil.

4. The sun warms the ground.

5. Baby turtles hatch.

6. Baby turtles crawl to the water.

Find the Babies

Draw a line from each mother to her baby. Color the pictures. [See page 99.]

Objective: To learn about the birth and growth of a crocodile.

Oscar, the Crocodile

This is the story of a crocodile that I call Oscar. I guess I can call him that since I've known him ever since he was born.

Now as everyone knows, you have to be careful around crocodiles. They're quick and they're rough. Where I live there are more crocodiles than people. In fact, I'm the only person who lives around here.

One hot night when the sun had just gone down, I was sitting on my porch watching the river roll by. All of the sudden I heard splashing! And I saw this big momma crocodile crawling out of the water. I stayed really quiet, 'cause I didn't want her to know I was around.

As I watched, she dug a hole in the sand by the river. Then she dropped some eggs in the hole and pushed the dirt in on top of them. Now have you ever seen a crocodile egg? ■ Well I can tell you that it's bigger than a chicken egg and it feels like the leather on a pair of shoes.

After she'd covered up the hole, mother crocodile turned around and crawled back into the water. I guess she'd waited till night to bury her eggs so no one would see what she was doing and know where to find them. Other reptiles and birds like to eat eggs!

A number of weeks passed. Then one day I was out on my porch again and I heard this soft grunting sound coming from the beach. Soon I saw mother crocodile hurry up to the spot where she'd dug the hole and, lo and behold, she started digging again. Soon she'd dug up three baby crocodiles and carried them one by one down to the water. The last one that she put in the muddy water I call Oscar. As far as I know, that's the last thing she had to do with any of her babies. Mother crocodiles usually don't bother taking care of babies once they're in the water.

Oscar did okay on his own. I watched him grow really fast during his first year. He went from a little crocodile you could hold in your hand to a great big long grown-up. Crocodiles can grow to be 23 feet long— that's longer than lots of boats!

Now at first no one was afraid of Oscar. He just bothered bugs and fish. But it wasn't long before he was eating birds and mice.

One day I saw him floating in the water with just his eyes showing. He looked asleep. My dog, Biscuit, walked over to the water to get a drink. Now Biscuit's smart. He kept an eye on Oscar. And it's a good thing he did because ... what do you think happened? ■ Right—Oscar zoomed out of the water and chased him. Biscuit ran up on my porch and started howling!

You know, Biscuit and I watch for Oscar every day now. Wouldn't you keep an eye on Oscar?

Oscar, the Crocodile

❑ Size Comparisons

To help children understand how long crocodiles are, have as many children as needed (approximately 6-8) to equal 23'-24' (the length of a large, present-day crocodile) lie on the floor head to toe. Use your measuring tape. If possible, take a picture of the children.

To really impress the youngsters, explain that the crocodiles that lived in the time of the dinosaurs grew to be 50' long. Have enough children to equal 50' lie on the floor, head to toe. Can you get them all in one picture?

❑ What Happened to Captain Hook?

If possible, read the story of *Peter Pan* to the children. (If you have access to a VCR, rent the movie of *Peter Pan* and show it.) Talk about why crocodiles and alligators are dangerous. [They have sharp teeth. They have powerful jaws and tails. They are very large. They are fast in water and on land.] Captain Cook learned not to get too close!

Jelly was a pink crocodile. He only ate cotton candy!

❑ Crocodile Tears

Explain to children that people sometimes say that someone "cried big old crocodile tears"—meaning that the person only pretended to be sad to trick someone else into helping them.

Cut out large tear shapes from colored construction paper. Give one to each child. Then help the children make up crocodile stories to write on their tear drops. [They can dictate them to you if they're too young to write.] Post all the tear drop stories on a bulletin board entitled *Crocodile Tears*.

❑ Crocodile Hand Play

After children have made the bag puppet on page 105, let them wear their puppets as you teach them this hand play.

Crocodile, crocodile, my oh my—	[Hand out in front of body throughout poem—rocking side to side as if gliding through water.]
See that birdie flying by?	[Look up at sky.]
Crocodile, crocodile, crunch, crunch—	[Make munching sounds. Open and shut puppet's mouth.]
Oops! I guess you swallowed lunch!	[Make swallowing sound.]

Science Sheet Notes

Crocodile Bag Puppet, page 105—Give each child a copy of this sheet and have him or her color the crocodile. Then have children paste the sheets onto construction paper and cut out the pieces along the heavy outlines. Give each child an unopened paper lunch bag. Help each child fold the bottom of the unopened bag in half. Staple the top snout to the top portion of the folded bag bottom. Staple the bottom snout to the lower portion of the folded bag bottom (within the fold). [See illustration.] Children can color the rest of their bags to match the colors they used on the snout. If desired, have children make teeth by cutting 10-12 1" triangles and pasting them around the top and bottom of the crocodiles's mouth. Add bean or button eyes.

Crocodile River, page 106—After children have listened to the story on page 102, give them this sheet to complete. Ask children to think of a name for their favorite crocodile on the page.

Crocodile Bag Puppet

See instructions on page 104.

Name _____

Crocodile River

Circle the crocodiles. Color the picture. [See page 104.]

How many crocodiles? _____

Fish

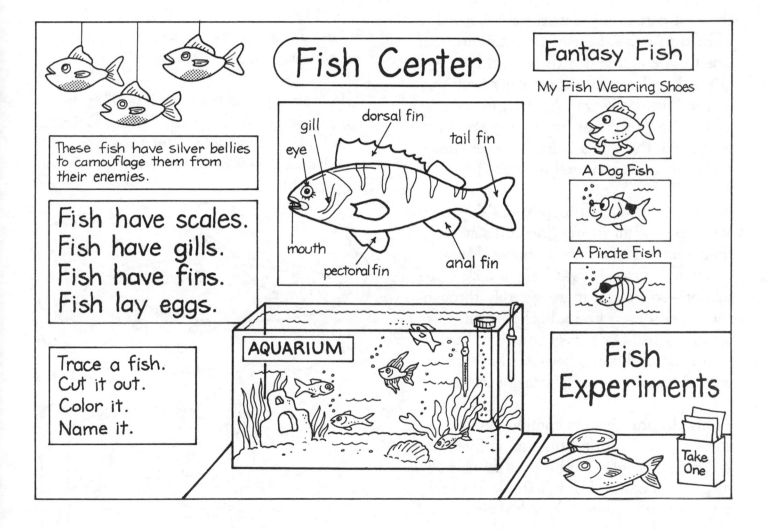

These fish have silver bellies to camouflage them from their enemies.

Fish have scales.
Fish have gills.
Fish have fins.
Fish lay eggs.

Trace a fish.
Cut it out.
Color it.
Name it.

Fish Center

gill
eye
dorsal fin
tail fin
mouth
pectoral fin
anal fin

AQUARIUM

Fantasy Fish

My Fish Wearing Shoes

A Dog Fish

A Pirate Fish

Fish Experiments

Take One

Objective: To learn that fish have scales, fins, gills, a backbone, ears, eyes, and a lateral line.

A Dream

Last night I had a wonderful dream. I was a fish! Scales covered my body, and I felt very smooth and slippery. I didn't have lungs anymore. I breathed through gills on each side of my head. And do you know what the best part of my dream was? When I wanted to move, I pushed my tail fin from side to side and glided through the water faster than I ever could with my feet! You see, my fish body was designed for swimming. I had fins on the top and bottom of me. All those fins helped me steer my body wherever I wanted it to go!

Before my dream, I thought all fish were the same shape. But in my dream, I saw fish that were lots of different shapes. I was a lucky fish because I was long and sleek like a salmon—so I could move speedily through the water. I even had a backbone, just like I do in my real body. Feel your backbone! Fish need backbones because that's what gives them their strong, straight shape.

In my dream, I was swimming along, enjoying the beautiful blue ocean, when suddenly I *heard* a loud sound! I was really surprised, because I didn't think fish had ears. But then I remembered: their ears are on the inside of their heads. I also remembered that fish have a great sense of smell. And in my dream I could smell every fish that swam by me. But I couldn't see them very well. That's because fish don't have very good eyesight. I was really shocked when I tried to close my eyes to go to sleep—fish don't have eyelids!

I began to wonder how I would know what was going on around me without seeing it. That's when I began to feel all kinds of sensations down the sides of my body. My mom had told me that a fish has something called a *lateral line* on its body. These lateral lines help fish feel everything that's happening in the water around them. Now my lateral line was feeling something huge coming toward me!

"Kyle, wake up! Time for breakfast!" It was mom, shaking me out of my dream. Whew! If she hadn't awakened me for breakfast, I think I might have been breakfast for a giant grouper fish!

A Fish

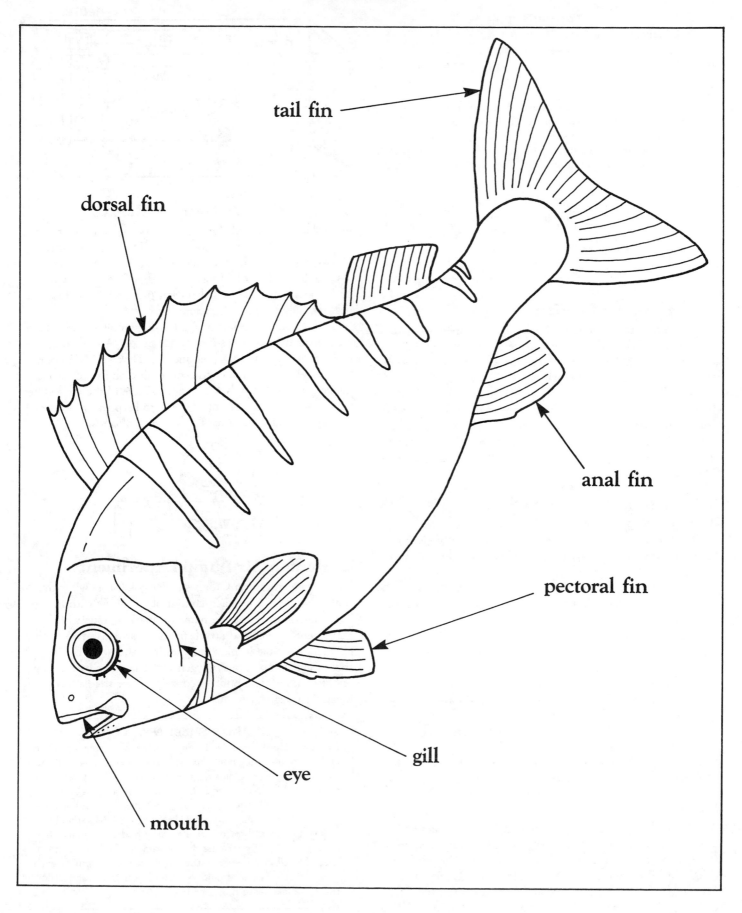

tail fin

dorsal fin

anal fin

pectoral fin

gill

eye

mouth

Vocabulary

gills—the organs, on each side of a fish's head, that allow the animal to breathe while swimming in water

fish scale—one of many flat, tiny, rigid plates covering the outside of a fish's body; a fish's skin

fins—the parts of a fish's body that help the animal steer, propel, and stay balanced in the water; akin to human arms and legs

backbone—an animal's spinal column. It gives the animal its straight shape.

lateral line—a line of special holes (or pores) along the side of a fish that helps it sense vibrations in the water

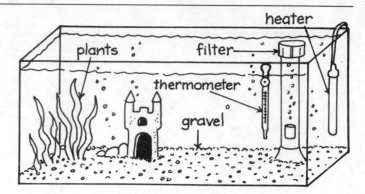

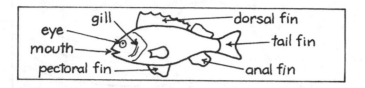

☐ Anatomy of a Fish

Draw a large version of the fish on page 109 on a big piece of oaktag. Label its parts. Then make a copy of page 109. White out the names of the parts on the copy and duplicate the page enough times for each child to have one. Have children look at the oaktag fish and copy the names of each part onto their pages. Have them color their fishes and write their names on the pages. Display the pictures in your fish center. [Give younger children copies of page 109 with labels in place. Help them learn to say, rather than write, the name of each part.]

☐ Setting Up An Aquarium

The best way to study an animal is to keep it as a pet. Setting up an aquarium can be an exciting and interesting learning experience for all. Here's what you need before you buy fish:

☐ **tank**—The number of fish dictates the size of the tank. Be sure that your tank has a large front window for children to look through.

☐ **heater**—You need one of these if it gets colder than 72° F in your room. Be sure to buy a new heater.

☐ **thermostat**—This item will help you select a water temperature.

☐ **thermometer**—This element will help you make sure your heater is operating properly.

☐ **gravel**—To anchor plants, add color, and catch debris, gravel is essential.

☐ **power filter**—This item will help keep water clean. Purchase a filter that hangs on the side of the tank.

☐ **air pump**—This item pumps oxygen into the water.

☐ **dipper**—This implement is used to pick up fish.

Visit a pet shop for books on aquariums and for information from salespersons. You may order fish and aquarium equipment through the mail from Carolina Biological Supply, Co. (2700 York Rd., Burlington, NC 27215; 1-800-334-5551). Setting up an aquarium is easy and well worth the time invested. Don't be intimidated! Jump in!

☐ Aquarium Activities Checklist

✔Display each part of the aquarium before you put the parts together. Ask children to examine (and touch) the parts. Discuss the role each part plays in an aquarium system.

✔On a large piece of white oaktag, draw a picture of your tank and all of its parts. Label each part and color the drawing. Display near the aquarium.

✔Conduct this experiment to show how a filter works: Place a coffee filter in a Melita-type coffee maker. Add used coffee grounds to a pitcher of water and stir. Have children pour the "dirty" water through the coffee filter and watch what happens to the grounds. Compare the role of the coffee filter to the way an aquarium filter works to keep water clean.

✔Make a feeding schedule for children to follow.

☐ Human Air Pump Experiment

Fill your aquarium tank (or a smaller goldfish bowl) with water. [No fish!] Give each child a plastic straw with his or her name on it. [Print the name on masking tape with a permanent marker and attach to the straw.] Ask two or three children at a time to blow bubbles into the tank. Explain that an air pump pumps oxygen into the water by blowing bubbles into it. The bubbles contain air for the fish to breathe through their gills!

Work Sheet Notes

My Fish Book, page 111—First, make a sample book for children to use as a guide. Cut along the dotted lines and staple the pages together. Color the fish on page 1 *yellow*. Color only the eye of the fish on page 2 *blue*. Color only the gills on page 3 *brown*. Color only the fins on page 4 *red*. Place the sample book on a tray with copies of page 111; a stapler; scissors; and red, yellow, blue, and brown crayons. Ask children to make their own fish books by looking at the sample. [Help children as needed.] Tell children that the word on the bottom of each page indicates what should be colored on that page. Allow them to make more than one book.

Name _____

My Fish Book

[See page 110.]

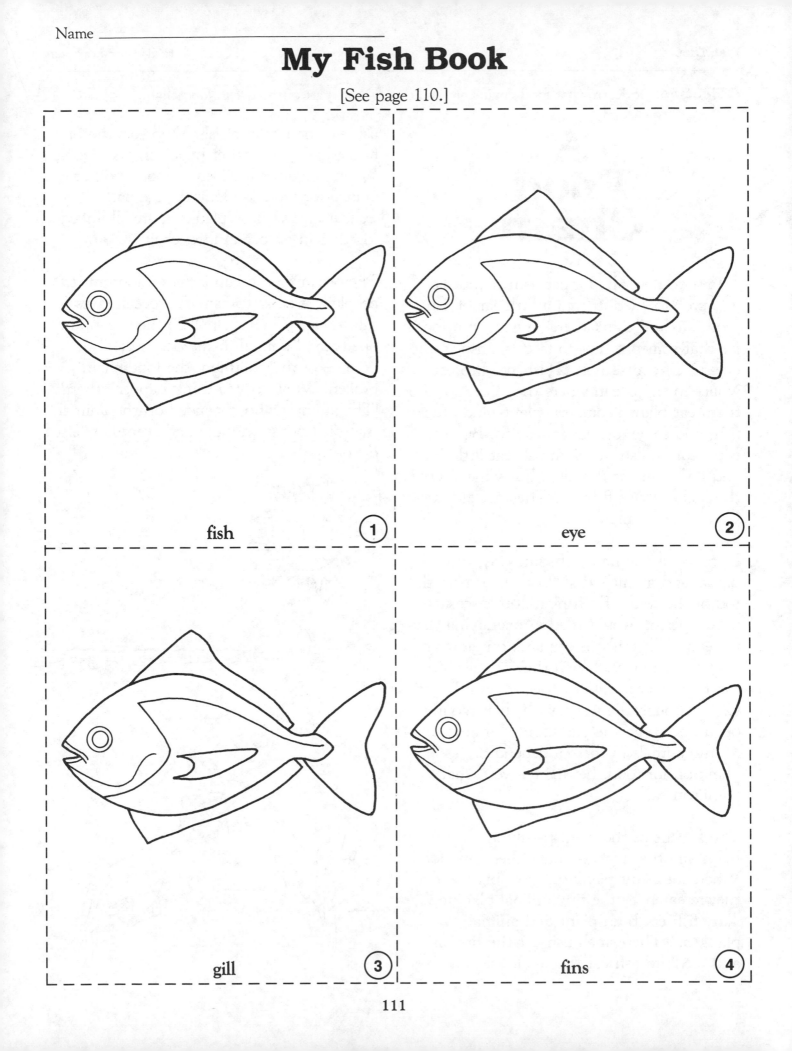

fish   1

eye   2

gill   3

fins   4

Objective: To learn what food chains are and that fish are part of the ocean food chain.

A Food Chain

Have you ever had a pet fish? If you did, you probably fed it from a little jar of fish food. Do you think there's a giant fish food jar that someone uses to feed the fish in the ocean? Of course not! ■ Fish need to eat what's in the ocean where they live. Some of them eat plants; some eat plants and other fish; and some just eat other fish. Big fish eat medium fish, medium fish eat little fish, and little fish eat tiny fish. But what do you think the tiniest fish eat? They eat *plankton*! Can you say "plankton"?

Plankton is the name of some tiny, tiny plants and animals that float on or near the top of the water. Each plankton is so small that a person would need a magnifying glass to see it. But millions of plankton grow and float in one place. When they are all together, they're easier to see. And fish just swim through the water with their mouths open and in go the plankton! Yummy! Many animals in the sea depend on plankton for food. Let me tell you what plankton eat.

The sun helps the plant plankton—just as it helps all other plants—make their own food. When the plant plankton grow big enough, they're eaten by the tiny animal plankton. Tiny fish eat both plant and animal plankton. Then small fish eat the tiny fish, and medium fish eat the small fish, and big

fish eat the medium fish. Who eats the big fish? (sharks and other huge fish and people) When one animal depends upon another animal for food, the animals are part of a *food chain*. Fish and plankton are all linked together in an ocean food chain.

The ocean food chain is very important to people as well as to fish. The ocean gives us fish to eat. When we pollute the ocean and one type of animal in the ocean dies out because of the pollution, the food chain is broken! What do you think happens then? [The animals who depended on the animal that died out go hungry and eventually also die out.]

Vocabulary

plankton—very small ocean plants and animals that drift with currents and are eaten by fish

food chain—the interdependence of animals and plants upon each other for food

❑ A Hands-on Food Chain

You need: 1 large fish, such as a blackfish or a striped bass
2 medium fish, such as flounder or bluefish
3 small fish, such as herring
1 large tray (or butcher paper)
lemon and paper towel for clean up

1 Hold up the large and the medium fish. Demonstrate how the big fish comes up behind the medium fish to eat it. Ask the children if they think the medium fish can eat the big fish? How many medium fish will a big fish eat at one meal?
2 Place the fish in the science center on a large tray or on a table covered with doubled butcher paper. Have children touch the fish. Let them show how the medium fish comes up behind the small fish to eat it, and how the large fish comes up behind the medium fish to eat it. Ask the children what the small fish will eat? (plankton) Have children clean their hands with lemon and paper towels.

[If you want to reuse the fish, put them in your school's freezer. Defrost a couple of hours before use.]

❑ Fish Checklist

✔ Who's bigger? Cut out several different sizes of cardboard fish. Place the fish in a basket and ask children to seriate according to size.
✔ Play magnetic *Go Fish*. Cut fifteen 4″ fish from oaktag. Place a paper clip on each of them. Write a number, a sight word, a letter, or a color on each fish. Drop the fish in a bowl. Hang a magnet ring on the end of a string tied to a dowel, and let children go fish! [Have children read the numbers, sight words, etc.]

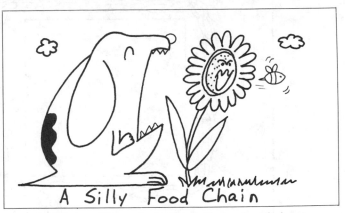

✔ Read "Fish" in *Where the Sidewalk Ends...* by Shel Silverstein.
✔ Make tuna fish sandwiches.
✔ Make a *silly food chain* with magazine pictures. For example, show a cow eating a cracker, a cracker eating a fish, a fish eating a sunflower seed, etc.
✔ Have children pantomime a big fish eating a medium fish, a medium fish eating a little fish, etc.

❑ Ocean Food Chain

You need: white oaktag and scissors
brushes and watercolor paints
paste
long piece of blue paper

1 Cut out of oaktag: 1 large fish (12″); 2 medium fish (6″); 5 little fish (3″); 10 tiny fish (1″); and some plankton. [Plankton can be small dots of colored paper from a hole punch.] Cut out a big circle for the sun.
2 Ask children to paint each fish with water colors. Paint the sun bright yellow.
3 Paste the fish onto a long piece of blue paper (as shown) and display in your fish center.

Science Sheet Notes

Ocean Food Chain, page 114—After children have listened to the story on page 112, give each child a copy of this page. Remind children that the sun helps plankton make food and the plankton become food for fish.

Number Fish, page 115—Use this sheet to help children practice counting to 20.

Ocean Food Chain

Color the pictures. Cut them out along the dotted lines.
Paste each picture in its spot in the food chain. [See page 113.]

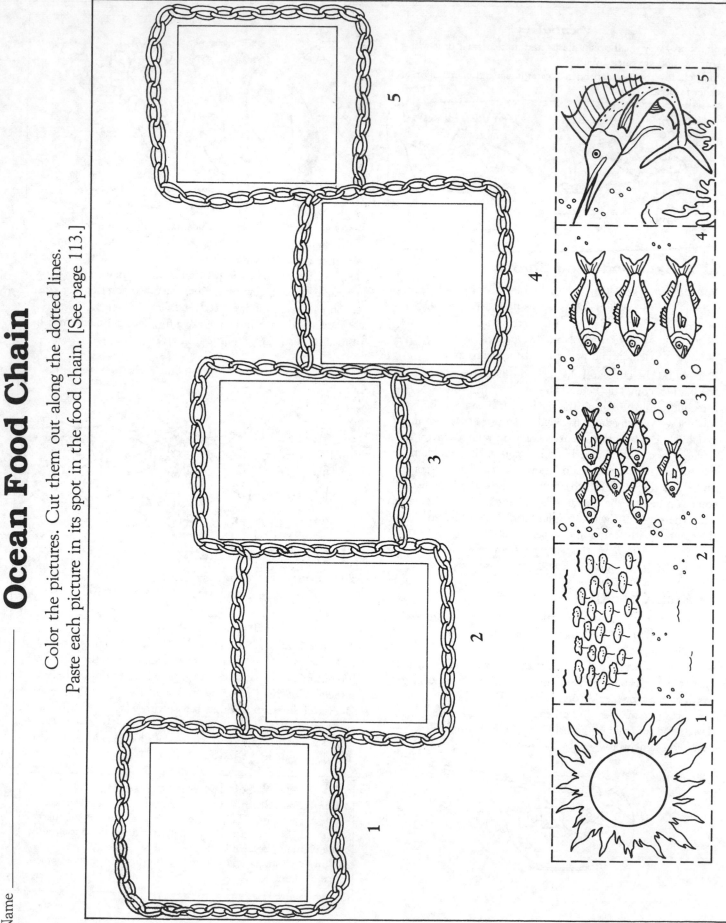

Name _____

Number Fish

Connect the dots from 1-20. Color the picture. [See page 113.]

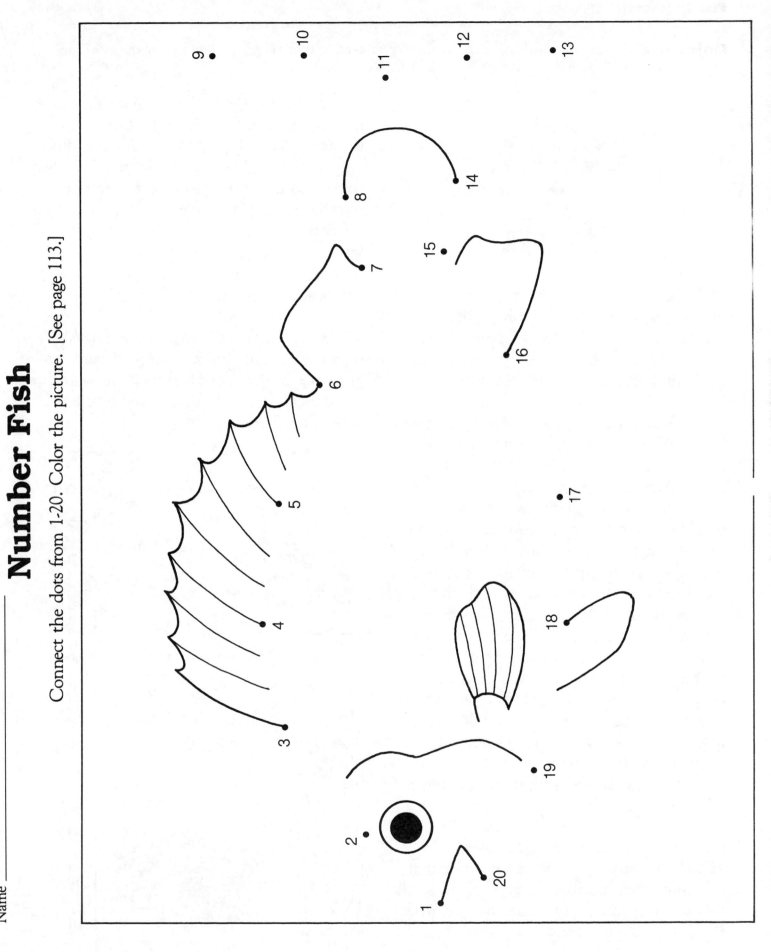

Objective: To learn that fish have many ways of protecting themselves, including: camouflage, swimming in schools, poison spines, etc.

To Catch A Fish

My name is Joey. I'm seven years old. And my favorite thing to do is fish. Some people say, "Fishing? That's boring!" Not to me, it isn't! I like to drop my hook in the water, sit back, and wait to see what happens.

When I was younger, I always wondered why I couldn't just jump in the water and catch a fish with my hands. So one day, while we were down by the water, my mom told me to try it. Wow! Those fish swam away so quickly, I didn't even get to touch one. So I decided I'd try to catch one with a net. I saw a big fish swimming toward some plants. I moved toward it, very quietly, and threw my net on top of it! All I caught was seaweed! The fish had hidden in the plants so well that I thought seaweed was a fish! My mom told me that the fish used the plants as *camouflage*. That means that the fish was able to hide because it was the same shape and color as the plants. That's when I realized that fish have some tricky ways of defending themselves against bigger animals (like me!) who want to catch them.

Have you ever heard of fish in school? ■ Well, a *school* is the name for a group of fish that swim together. Lots of times, small fish swim in schools to make their enemies think they are one big fish.

My cousin, Jesse, who lives in Hawaii, told me that tropical fish (those are fish that live in warm places) have special ways of protecting themselves. Often they are very brightly colored so that they can hide among the colorful ocean plants. He also told me that a few fish—such as the lion fish—have pointed spines all over their bodies. These spines have poison on them. When an enemy gets too close, it gets stuck!

My favorite fish is the flying fish! That's because it swims so fast that it actually can jump out of the water and glide through the air to escape its enemies! I would love to be able to do that!

116

Vocabulary

school—a large number of fish, porpoises, or whales that feed and travel together

camouflage—When an animal's body covering (feathers, hair, scales, etc.) is similar in color to the surroundings that the animal lives in, we say that one of the animal's natural defenses is camouflage.

❏ Where's Swimmy?

You need: *Swimmy*, a book by Leo Lionni
5′ sheet of brown butcher paper
pencil
6 3″-sponge fish, cut from household sponges
red paint in a bowl
black paint, slightly diluted, in tray

1 Discuss the reasons that fish swim in schools. (because they look like one big fish, because there is safety in numbers, etc.) Then read *Swimmy* to the children and ask children how the fish in the story were protected by swimming in a school.

2 Place the butcher paper on a large table or on the floor. Draw a large pencil outline of a fish on the paper.

3 Dip one sponge fish in red paint and press it inside the fish outline on the paper, at the position of the fish's eye. The red fish is Swimmy! Title the paper: *Where's Swimmy?*

4 Ask two children at a time to dip sponges in black paint and press them on the space inside the fish shape.

5 Display the completed Swimmy mural where children can touch the fish and count them—and, of course, find Swimmy!

❏ Gyotaku

Gyotaku is the Japanese art of fish printing.

You need: an ink roller or paint brush
poster paints
a whole fish
white painting paper

1 Use the ink roller to roll a light coating of paint onto the fish. [You may also brush paint on.]

2 Gently press the white paper over the painted fish. Lift it off the fish carefully and place it on a table to dry.

3 Display finished gyotakus in your fish center!

❏ Flying Fish

This activity is wonderful for outdoors or inside a large room.

You need: 2 medium-sized balloons per child
yarn or string
masking tape
black markers

1 Blow up each child's balloons. [If children are able, let them blow up their own balloons.] Tie balloons with loose knots or with pieces of yarn or string.

2 Cut a 5″ piece of masking tape for each balloon. Fold the tape lengthwise and stick it to the top of the balloon. This is the *dorsal fin.*

3 Show children how to make the eyes, mouth, and gills on each fish with the black marker.

4 Let the fish fly! Just untie the loose knot and hold the fish up high. Hold *Flying Fish Races* to see whose fish can fly the longest amount of time or fly the farthest distance.

❏ Silver Bellies

You need: brown butcher paper and marker
scissors and stapler
newspaper (shredded)
paints and brushes
glue
silver glitter (in shaker can or large bowl)
string or yarn
tacks

1 Ask children if they've noticed that all fish have silver bellies. When something swimming under a fish looks up, the silver belly is hard to see because it looks like it's part of the shimmering silver water.

2 Fold a 15″ piece of butcher paper in half. Draw a fish shape that's about 7″ long on one side of the fold. Cut out the shape. You now have two brown fish. Staple the two fish shapes together along one side and on both ends. Stuff newspaper into the fish and then staple the open side closed. Paint the top half of the fish. Add eyes. Let the paint dry.

3 Cover the bottom portion of the fish with glue. Sprinkle the bottom with silver glitter (or dip it into a bowl of glitter). Set the fish upside down to let the glue dry.

4 Put a string through the top of each fish. Hang all the fish from your ceiling with tacks.

Science Sheet Notes

Fish Defenses, page 118—After children have colored the pictures on this science sheet, have them cut along the dotted lines. Show them how to fold the cutout into quarters so that page 1 is the first page in the book.

Find the Hidden Fish, page 119—Discuss camouflage with the children. Then give them this science sheet to complete.

Fish Defenses

Color each picture. Cut along the dotted lines. Fold the cutout to make a minibook.
[See page 117.]

3. Some fish have spines.

2. Some fish can fly.

Name

How do fish defend themselves?

4. Some fish can hide.

1. Fish travel in schools.

Find the Hidden Fish

Circle all the fish. Color the picture. [See page 117.]

Objective: To learn that fish live in all types of water.

Sparky Speaks

My name is Sparky, and I'm a talking fish. Since I've never met another fish that could talk I only get to tell my stories to people. The story I want to tell you today is about water. Now everyone knows that fish live in water, and they've lived in water for millions of years. My ancestors, in fact, swam in water the dinosaurs walked in!

Did you know there are two main kinds of water? Salt water and fresh water. Fresh water doesn't have salt in it. What do you think salt water has in it? (salt) ■ All of my family—my cousins and aunts and uncles— live in the ocean, where the water is salty. But there are other fish who live in lakes and rivers where the water doesn't have salt in it. Sunfish, perch, and trout, for example, like to swim in clean streams and rivers. They can't live in salt water. Some catfish also only live in fresh water, but they have cousin catfish that only live in salt water. By the way, can you guess why catfish are called catfish? [They have whiskers like a cat's.]

■ The ocean—which is all salt water—is cold in some places and warm in other places. Some of the world's most beautiful fish— such as parrotfish, angelfish, and zebrafish— like to live only in the warm places. But bluefish, snapper, and mackerel like the cooler places best.

I used to think that all salt-water fish always stayed in salt water, and that all fresh-water fish stayed in fresh water. Then I found out about the salmon and the eel. These fish are special. The salmon lives in the ocean, but swims to fresh-water rivers to lay its eggs. The eel does just the opposite. Eels live in fresh water, but swim thousands of miles to lay their eggs in the ocean's salt water. What interesting fish!

There are many other interesting things to learn about the waters that fish live in. Just read some books about us. Until later, this is your friend, Sparky, saying "So long!"

Vocabulary

cold-blooded—When an animal's body temperature changes with the temperature of its environment, the animal is cold-blooded.

warm-blooded—When an animal's body temperature is always the same, the animal is warm-blooded.

☐ A Cold-Blooded Experiment

A fish's body temperature is close to the temperature of the water in which it lives. A fish that lives in warm water will have a warmer body temperature than a fish that lives in cold water. [People always have the same body temperature—no matter where they live.] The following experiment is a hands-on way of explaining what is meant by *cold-blooded*.

You need: 2 small, clear fish bowls
warm and cold water
2 small sponge fish, cut from household sponges

1 Fill one fish bowl with very warm water and the other bowl with cold water.

2 Drop one sponge fish into each bowl. Ask a child to take the fish out of the bowls. Which fish feels hot and which one feels cold?

3 Explain that real fish, just like these sponge fish, feel cold in cold water and warm in warm water.

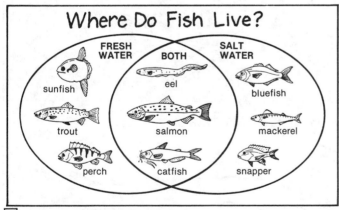

Where Do Fish Live?

FRESH WATER: sunfish, trout, perch
BOTH: eel, salmon, catfish
SALT WATER: bluefish, mackerel, snapper

☐ Where Do We Live?

You need: marker
large piece of paper
copies of page 122
crayons and scissors
paste

1 Make two overlapping circles on the paper. Label the circles, as shown, and title the chart *Where Do Fish Live?*

2 Give children copies of page 122. Ask them to color and cut out the fish.

3 Have children paste the fish in the appropriate categories on the paper. Be sure to provide lots of help.

4 Display the completed chart in your fish center.

☐ A Salt-water Experiment

You need: 2 large plastic cups
cool water
2 teaspoons salt

1 Fill each cup halfway with water. Have the child taste the water in each glass. Is there any difference?

2 Add 2 teaspoons of salt to one glass of water. Stir vigorously. What happens to the salt?

3 Have the child taste each glass of water again. Are they different now? Why?

☐ A Classroom Ocean

Turn your dramatic play area into an undersea world!

You need: brown paper bags
newspaper
stapler and masking tape
paints and brushes
butcher paper
colored cellophane (or plastic wrap)

1 **Rocks.** Stuff the bags with newspaper. Staple or tape the bags closed and paint them to look like rocks. Place the rocks near the ocean scene.

2 **Ocean scene.** Cover a wall with a long piece of butcher paper. Paint an ocean scene on it using blue, green, and brown paints. Tear long strips of cellophane (to resemble seaweed) and tape them to the butcher paper. If desired, add fish to the painting.

3 **Play.** After the area is complete, have children pretend that they are living underwater. How does it feel? What do they see? Record answers on an experience chart.

☐ Fish Poster

You need: large piece of oaktag
black marker
fish-shaped stencils, cut from cardboard
crayons or colored markers

A fish needs clean water to grow…

1 Ask children why they think fish need to live in clean water. List their ideas and your own on the oaktag.

2 Lay the oaktag chart on the art table, and ask children to use the stencils to make fish tracings all around the edges of the poster. Have them color the tracings.

3 Display the finished poster on your door for other classes and friends to see.

Science Sheet Notes

Fish in the Water, page 122—After children have listened to "Sparky Speaks" on page 120, give them this sheet to complete. Remind them that most fish live either in fresh water or salt water. Only a few fish can survive in both kinds of water.

Tropical Fish, page 123—Explain to children that many of the fish people keep as pets are tropical fish. That's because these fish are beautifully colored. Give children this sheet to help them with counting skills.

Name _____

Fish in the Water

[See page 121.]

Color these fresh-water fish yellow.

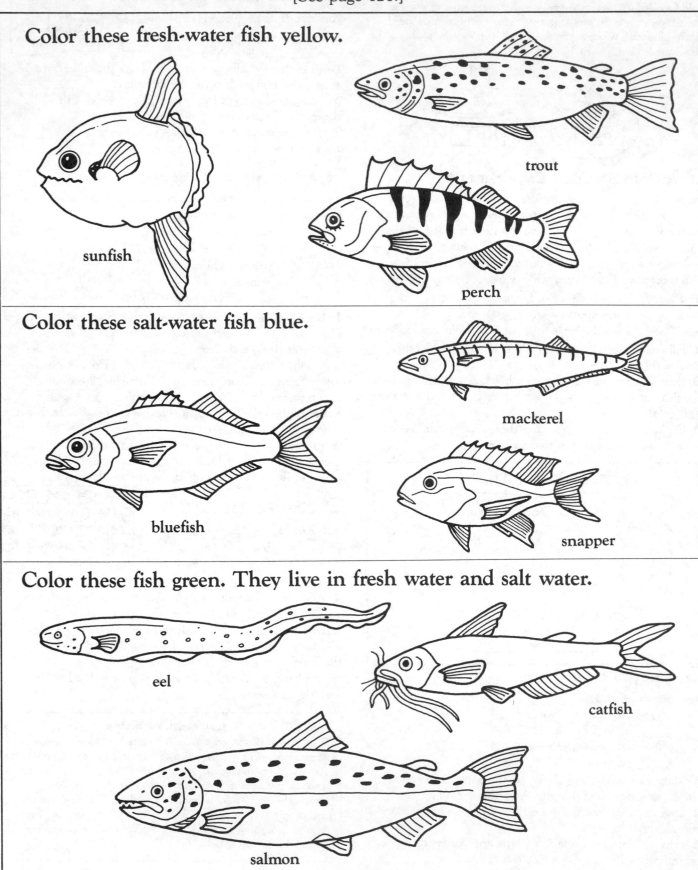

sunfish

trout

perch

Color these salt-water fish blue.

mackerel

bluefish

snapper

Color these fish green. They live in fresh water and salt water.

eel

catfish

salmon

Name _____

Tropical Fish

Count the fish in each row. Write how many in the box. [See page 121.]

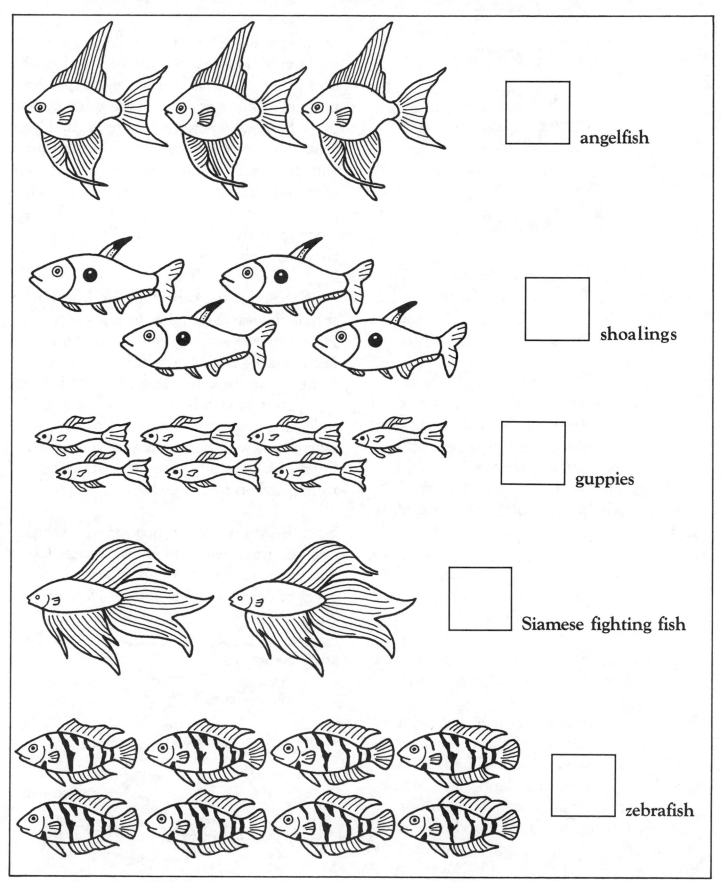

angelfish

shoalings

guppies

Siamese fighting fish

zebrafish

Objective: To learn that most fish lay eggs, that some fish bear live young, and that some fish migrate to lay their eggs.

Where Do Fish Come From?

Most fish have babies by laying eggs. As the mother fish swims along, she drops the eggs into the water under her. Then she usually just swims away. The eggs hatch on their own.

Some fish *do* stay around to take care of their babies until they hatch. A brook trout builds a stone nest for its eggs. Sea catfish fathers carry eggs in their mouths until the babies hatch. By the way, do you know what a newly-hatched baby fish is called? (a fry)

■Some fish do not lay eggs. Shark babies are born alive. Sometimes as many as twenty shark babies are born at once! Guppies are tropical fish that can have as many as 100 live babies at one time! How would you like to have that many brothers and sisters?

■There are two kinds of fish that swim thousands of miles each year to have babies. One of these fish is a *salmon*. Baby salmon are always born in little fresh-water ponds. Soon after the salmon babies hatch from eggs, they swim out of the pond into a stream. The stream becomes a big river, and the river carries the salmon backwards to a

big ocean. It's like riding a roller coaster backwards! The salmon live, eat, and grow up in the ocean. After a while, the grown-up salmon know that it is time to go back to the little pond where they were born. They leave the ocean and swim back up the river, with the water pushing against them. It is a long and difficult trip. Finally, the salmon get back to their little pond and lay the eggs. They want their babies to be born where they were born.

Now the *eel* is the other kind of fish that travels thousands of miles to lay its eggs. Have you ever seen an eel? It's long and thin like a snake—but it's a fish! Eels usually live in fresh-water streams. But when it's time to lay eggs, mother eels swim thousands of miles underwater to the special ocean place where they were born. Baby eels are always born in salty ocean water. Grown-up eels usually live in fresh water.

Scientists do not know how or why salmon and eels travel so far to lay their eggs. Could you find your way through thousands of miles of ocean without a map? How do you think these fish do it?

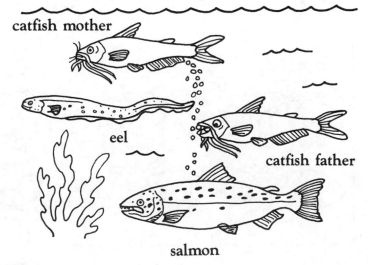

catfish mother

eel

catfish father

salmon

Vocabulary

spawn—to lay eggs; a term used in regard to fish

❑ A Fish-egg Snack

Purchase an inexpensive jar of caviar ($5 or less) at your local market. Place the caviar on a dish. Tell the children that the dish holds fish eggs. Ask children to look at the eggs with a magnifier. Have them smell and touch the caviar. At snack time, put the eggs on crackers for an interesting taste treat.

❑ Fish Dough

Have children make little fish eggs from dough or modeling clay. Then ask them to make clay models of the fish from which the eggs came. Ask children the names of their fish. Display each set of eggs and fish on an individual piece of cardboard with a description written at the bottom.

❑ Big Book Fish

Children love to read big books, and they will have lots of fun helping to write their own! Place large painting paper on a chart or easel stand. [Thick paper is best.] Ask children to help you write and illustrate a story about a fish fry.

❑ Does It Lay Eggs?

You need: large piece of paper
pictures of egg-laying animals (from this book or from magazines)
wide-tipped black marker
paste

1 Discuss the animals, including fish, that lay eggs: reptiles, birds, amphibians, insects, and spiders.

2 At the top of your paper, write the title *Does It Lay Eggs?* Paste pictures of the egg-laying animals you've discussed on the paper.

3 Have children draw, color, and cut out egg shapes. Paste the shapes around the pictures on the chart.

❑ Fishy Stories

Have children dictate stories about mother fish. Ask: "Where did the mother spawn? How many eggs were laid? How many fry hatched? What did the baby fish look like? Where did the fry go after they hatched?"

Write the stories on white drawing paper and have the children illustrate them.

Science Sheet Notes

Ocean Maze, page 126—Remind children that baby fish are called *fry*. Then give them this science sheet to complete.
On Our Way Home, page 127—Review the details of how salmon return to the ponds they were born in to lay their eggs. Then give children this science sheet.

Ocean Maze

Draw a line from the mommy fish to the baby fish. Do not go over any lines. [See page 125.]

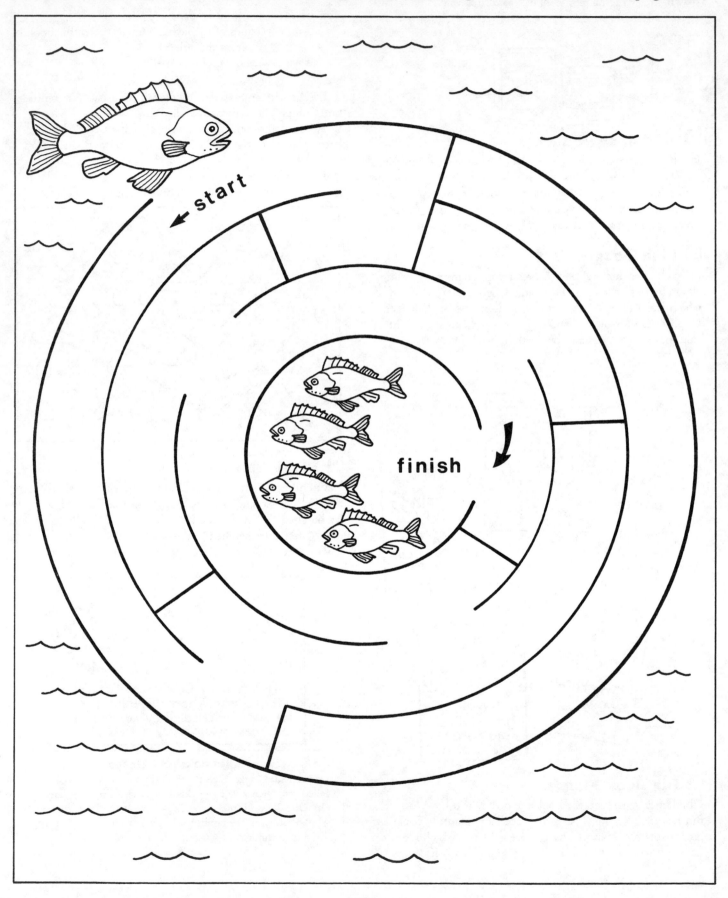

start

finish

Name _____

On Our Way Home

Color the water. Cut out the salmon. Glue them in the stream, swimming to the pond. [See page 125.]

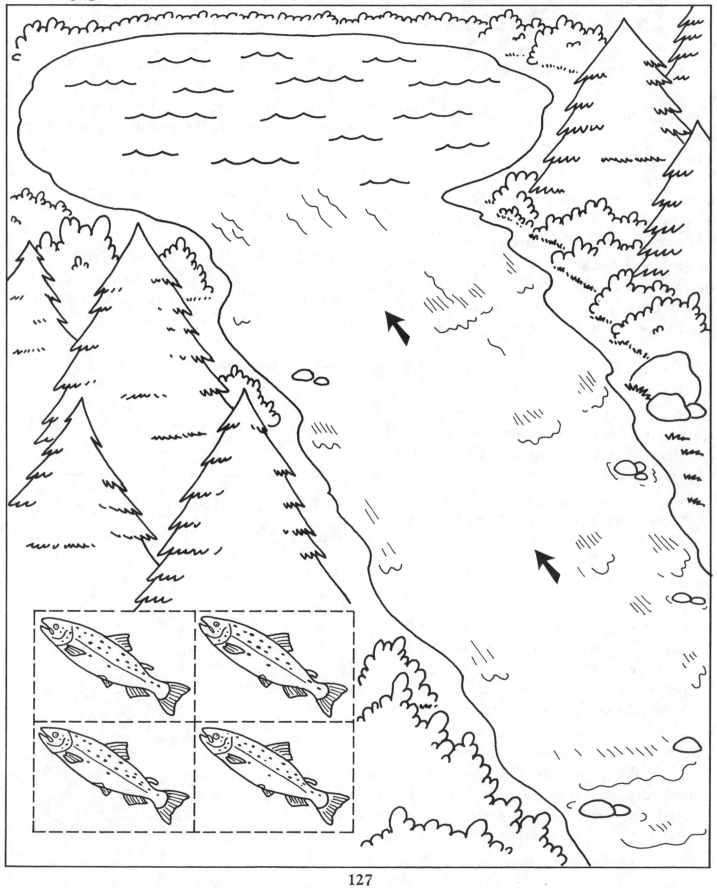

Objective: To learn about sharks!

Sh-Sh-Sh-Shark!

I want to tell you something I've never told anyone before. When I was small, I was very afraid of sharks. It's true! Sometimes I would be so frightened that I wouldn't want to take a bath or swim in the ocean. Then my friend gave me a book about sharks. Did you know that sharks come in all different sizes? The dwarf shark is only as big as my hand, but the whale shark is as big as three school buses put together! Most kinds of sharks are about the size of my daddy.

I always wondered where sharks live. Can a shark live in a swimming pool or a bathtub? (of course not) ■ Sharks live everywhere in the ocean. They have to keep swimming all the time—they can never stop because if they do, they'll sink!

Have you ever seen a picture of a shark's teeth? ■ They are very sharp and there are lots of them! When I lost my baby teeth, my grown-up teeth grew in. That's all the teeth I'll ever have. But sharks are lucky. If a shark looses a tooth, a new one grows in—even if the shark looses the same tooth twenty times! Here's another interesting thing I found out in the book: the scales on a shark's body are like tiny teeth.

Sharks are always hungry and they are always looking for food. They have long, sleek bodies that help them swim quickly through the water to catch other fish. Sharks eat all kinds of animals that live in the water. I felt a lot better when I found out that they don't really like to eat people!

There are many types of sharks, but my favorite is the great white shark. It has teeth as long as your fingers, and it is the most dangerous of all sharks. It always swims with its mouth open—anything that goes in the mouth gets swallowed. Scientists cut open one great white shark and found old shoes and a tire inside!

The great white shark lives where the water is very deep and cold. It travels alone except for some pilot fish who hang around to eat the leftovers from its dinners.

Since I've read and learned so much about sharks, I'm not afraid of them anymore. In fact, when I grow up I'd like to become an *ichthyologist*. That's a person who studies fish. Don't you think that would be fun?

Great White Shark

128

The Great White Shark

Vocabulary
ichthyologist—a scientist who studies fish

❑ **Shark Paintings**

Cut a pad of your large painting paper into the shape of a shark. [Use the shark on page 129 as a guide.] Place the pad where children can take sheets from it to use during painting time. Display their art/shark work around the room.

❑ **Anatomy of a Shark**

Enlarge the picture of the shark from page 129 on a piece of white oaktag. Label it's parts, and hang it in your fish center or on a *Shark* bulletin board.

❑ **Sand Shark Pet**

A sand shark is a good aquarium pet and is easy to find in pet shops. Set up an aquarium (as described on page 110). Instead of putting tropical fish in the aquarium, put in sand sharks. Ask children to observe the sharks' behavior, characteristics, and eating habits. [Consult with pet shop personnel regarding proper water conditions for your sand shark.]

> Hammerhead Shark
> Great White Sharks
> Dwarf Shark

❑ **Shark Study Groups**

Borrow books about sharks from your library. [The National Wildlife Federation publishes lovely shark books.] Put the books in your classroom library for free-time reading. Let children with similar interests form groups to learn more about their favorite sharks.

❑ **Make A Shark Book!**

You need: long sheets of painting paper
long sheets of construction paper
markers or crayons

1 Book pages. Cut four sheets of long painting paper into the shape of a shark for the inside of the book.
2 Book cover. Cut a shark-shaped cover from construction paper, and staple the cover on top of the book pages.
3 Story. Have the child write (or dictate) a shark fact for each page of the book. Ask the child to illustrate the fact on each page. [Younger children can just draw a shark on each page and color it.]

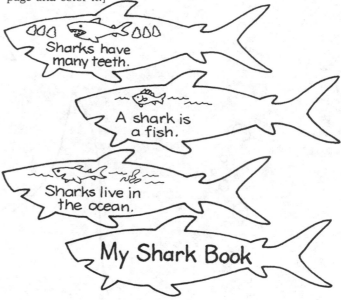

❑ **Shark Stencils**

Cut 5"-7" shark stencils out of cardboard. [Use the shark on page 129 as a guide.] Place the stencils in the science area or at the art table for children to use in making books, pictures, and posters.

Science Sheet Notes

Shark Friends, page 131—Remind children that there are many different kinds of sharks. Then give them this sheet to complete.

Shark Stick Puppets, page 132—Have each child paste a copy of this page onto construction paper, color the sharks, and then cut them out. Paste cutouts onto craft sticks. Let children "swim" their sharks around the room.

Shark Friends

Cut out the pictures along the dotted lines. Paste each cutout shark next to the shark it matches. [See page 130.]

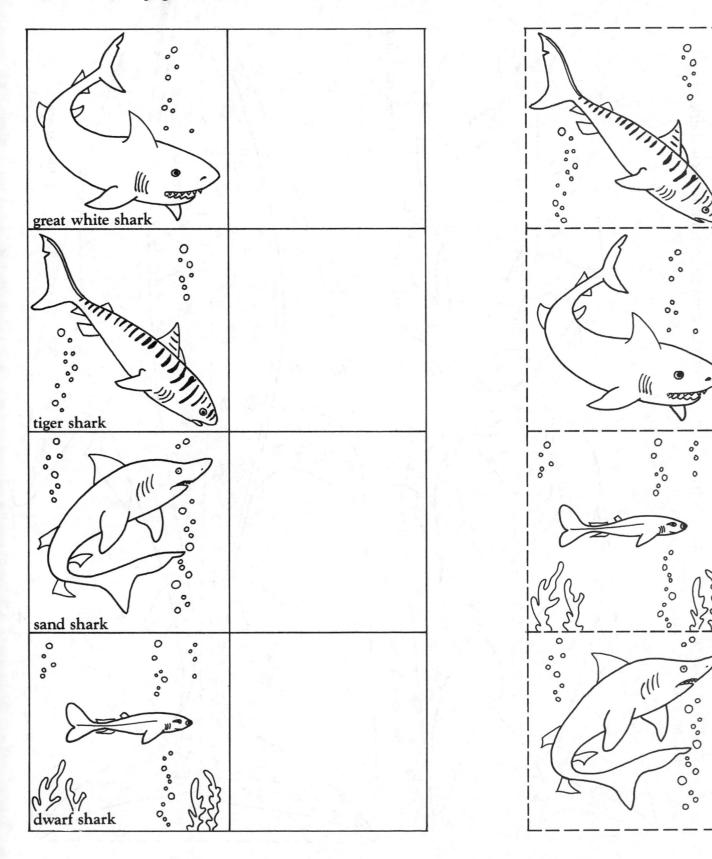

great white shark

tiger shark

sand shark

dwarf shark

Name _____

Shark Stick Puppets

Paste this page onto construction paper. Color and cut out the pictures. Paste each shark to a craft stick. [See page 130.]

hammerhead shark

megamouth shark

whale shark

Birds

The Bird Center

All About Birds
A bird has feathers.
A bird has 2 wings.
A bird has 2 feet.
A bird can fly.

Pictures of Birds

People learn how to make airplanes by studying birds.

Amazing Bird Facts
The peregrine falcon can dive to the ground at 180 mph.

Feather Facts
Flight feathers help birds fly.
Down feathers keep us warm.

Science Shelf
How is a robin's nest made?

Compare the eggs:
chicken
ostrich
quail

Matching the feathers

Waterproof Feathers

Our Reading Nest
Come in. Sit and read a book about birds.

Objective: To learn that birds have feathers, wings, and two feet.

Who Grows Feathers?

bee hummingbird

ostrich

Only one kind of animal in the whole world grows feathers. Guess who? ■ All birds have feathers and all birds have wings. What do they use their wings for? ■ Right—they use them mainly for flying. Birds that fly travel faster from place to place than any other kind of animal.

Birds come in many shapes and sizes. After all, there are almost 9000 different kinds of birds in the world. The smallest bird is the bee hummingbird—he's about as big as your hand. The biggest bird is the ostrich. He'd probably bump his head coming through your doorway. He's 8 feet tall—that's taller than most grown-up people.

All birds have two legs and feet, but most birds don't use their feet for walking. They mainly use them to grab onto tree limbs or for hopping from place to place as they look for food on the ground.

Are there any kinds of birds that can't fly? ■ Yes! For example, ostriches and penguins can't fly, but they still get around quite well. An ostrich can outrun a person and a penguin can swim much faster and for a much longer time than most people!

Think about this question: "How did people learn to make airplanes and helicopters?" ■ Well, if you wanted to learn to make a flying machine, you'd probably study things that fly. And that's just what people did—they studied the way birds fly. Flying is one of the many things we've learned to do by studying the animals in our world.

Anatomy of a Bird

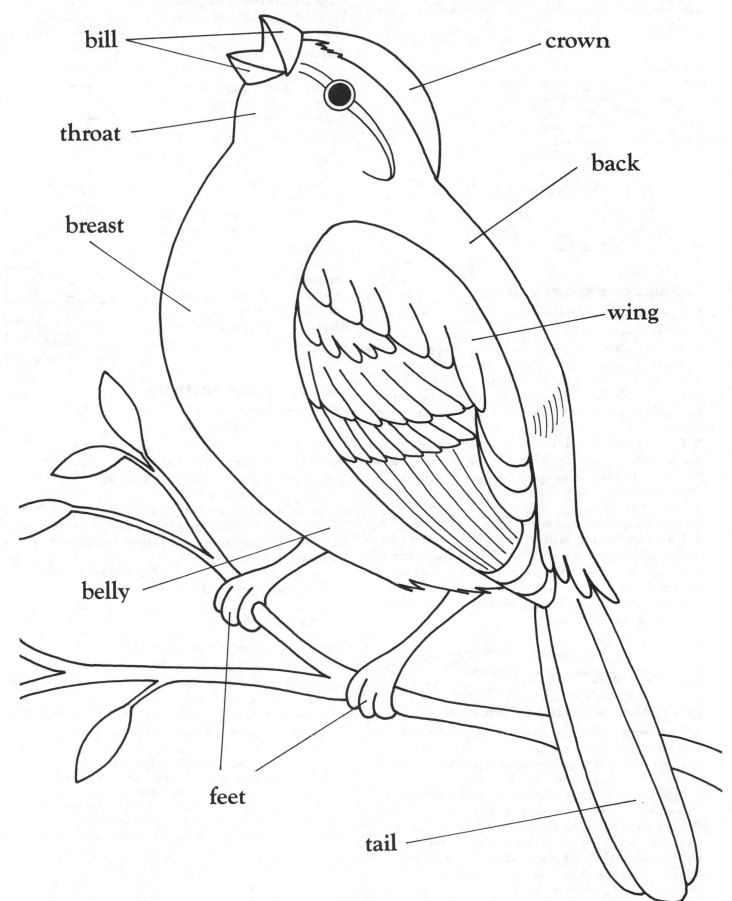

bill

crown

throat

back

breast

wing

belly

feet

tail

Vocabulary

flight feathers—the outer feathers that cover the wings and tail of the bird

contour feathers—the curved feathers that cover the body of the bird

down feathers—the small, soft feathers found beneath the outer feathers of ducks, geese, and other waterfowl

preen gland (also called uropygial gland)—a gland at the base of the tail feathers from which a bird gets oil to spread over its feathers to keep them waterproof

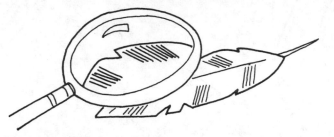

❑ Feather Exploration

You need: flight and down feathers
magnifying glass

1 Feel the feathers. Let children handle a few feathers. Are they light or heavy? Explain that because feathers are so light, they make it easy for a bird to stay in the air.

2 Look closely. Let children look at a flight feather through a magnifying glass. Can they see how tightly the parts of the feather connect?

3 Float a feather in air. Let children compare the speeds at which a feather falls compared to a rock, a pencil, a ball, etc. Have each child hold a feather in one hand and another object in the other hand. Ask children to predict which item will hit the ground first when dropped at the same time. Then let the experiments begin!

4 Float a feather in water. Let children experiment with feathers and water. Will the feathers float? Will they keep the bird dry? Explain that birds have preen glands. Birds spread oil from these glands over their feathers to make them waterproof. [Let children spread petroleum jelly over feathers and then dip them in water.]

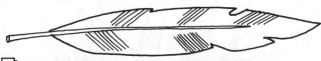

❑ Feather Activities Checklist

✔Give children a variety of feathers. Have them classify the feathers by size, shape, or color.

✔Collect feathers. Glue onto oaktag. If possible, label each feather with the name of the bird it came from.

✔Display several feathers (that match in color and shape) from each of 3-4 different birds. Mix the feathers up and ask the children to put matching feathers together.

✔Cut large wings from construction paper. Cover the wings with feathers. Attach wings with string to a child's back.

✔Make a feather necklace. Make beads from clay. String onto yarn. Stick feathers in clay.

❑ Feathered Airplanes

Have children work with you at a table as you make these paper airplanes.

You need: paper, scissors, stapler
feathers and glue

1 Fold a piece of paper in half lengthwise. Then reopen.
2 On one end, fold the two corners in until they meet at the center.
3 Fold the folded corners again to meet at the center.
4 Now fold the paper in half again—with the earlier folds inside. Staple through all folds by placing a staple midway in the length of the paper, about $^1/_2$″ in from the center fold.
5 Fold back the wings and cut the point off the tip. Have children glue a few feathers on the wings and then put the planes into service!

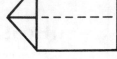
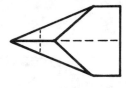

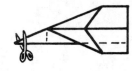

❑ Color Some Feathers

You need: down feathers
food coloring

1 Explain to children that people have used feathers— especially down—for as long as anyone can remember: for pillows, because feathers are soft; and for decorations, because feathers are pretty.

2 Set out several bowls of food coloring and a bag of down feathers. Let each child have a feather to dip in each color. Have the child place the dipped feathers to dry on a sheet of paper with his or her name.

3 Let children decorate their finished Bird Parts Puzzles (page 137) with their dyed feathers.

Sources: Feathers

Here are our recommendations for getting feathers:

❑ Take a nature walk with the children. Look for fallen nests.

❑ Buy feathers at an arts and crafts store or a bridal accessories shop.

❑ Visit a zoo, pet store, or poultry farm and ask for feathers.

❑ Open a down pillow and remove the feathers you need.

Science Sheet Notes

Bird Parts Puzzle, page 137—Have children cut apart the puzzle along the dotted lines and paste the pieces on construction paper to create the picture of the stork. Remind children that all birds have a bill, two legs, and feathers.

Name _____

Bird Parts Puzzle

Cut along the dotted lines. Put the pieces together to make the picture of a bird.
[See page 136.]

stork

137

Objective: To learn that birds have no teeth and that birds eat different kinds of food—primarily fruits and/or seeds, insects, fish, or small animals.

Dinner with My Bird Friends

One day I invited all of my bird friends for dinner. Having birds over for dinner can be tricky because birds have no teeth. You have to have exactly the kind of food they are used to eating—or they'll go hungry. Here's a list of the birds I invited to my dinner party.

The sparrow, who sometimes lives in the forest and sometimes in the city, loves to eat all kinds of seeds. So I had sunflower, corn, and sesame seeds for him.

The toucan, who looks a lot like a parrot with his brightly colored feathers, lives in the jungle. His favorite meal is fresh fruit—papayas and mangoes and bananas. Yum, yum, yum!

The woodpecker likes to eat little bugs. Where do you think Woodpecker lives? (in a hollow tree in the forest) ■I served Woodpecker a dish of earthworms and spiders!

Mother Pelican loves the taste of fish. She lives close to the water because she hardly ever eats anything that doesn't come from the sea. I gave her some tuna. What would you have fed Pelican?

■The hawk and owl are hunters. They like to eat rats and snakes and sometimes other birds! Most of their neighbors are pretty careful around them. I asked these two to bring their own food!

If you had bird friends over for dinner, which birds would you invite? ■What would you feed them?

❏ Feeding Time

1 Field trips. Plan a field trip to a zoo or pet store with the children. Call ahead so that you can arrive at a time when the birds are being fed.

2 Bird feeders. Feeders are a good way to attract birds for youngsters to observe. Before you build one of the feeders described on this page, buy one of the inexpensive bird guides listed under *Resources* and, if your budget allows, a pair of inexpensive binoculars. These items will make watching the birds that dine at your feeder a truly entertaining and educational experience.

❏ Pinecone Feeder

You need: string, pinecone, knife, peanut butter

Tie a string around the base of the pinecone. Use a knife to press peanut butter all over the cone. [Explain to children that peanuts are seeds, and birds that like seeds will eat the peanut butter.] Hang the cone from a tree limb and watch!

❏ Milk Carton Feeder

You need: hole puncher or knife; empty, clean milk carton; string or yarn; bird seed

Punch a hole in the top of the empty carton (as shown), and thread string or yarn through it. Cut out the center portion of each side panel, leaving about a 1″ frame all around. Put bird seed in the bottom of the carton. Hang your feeder outside.

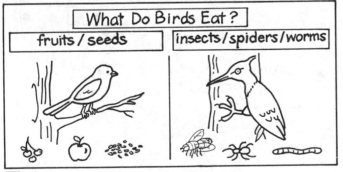

❏ Bird Food Bulletin Board

You need: yarn
  light-colored construction paper
  marker
  magazines and scissors
  tacks
  (optional) bird seed and tweezers

1 Preparing the board. Use yarn to divide a bulletin board into two sections. On each of three strips of construction paper, use a marker to write one of the following: fruits/seeds, insects/spiders/worms, and What Do Birds Eat? Place the strips on the board as shown.

2 Filling the board. Find at least one picture of each of the birds described below (or enlarge the pictures on page 138 and cut them out). Post each picture in the appropriate section of the board.
- ❏ *insect specialist* (woodpecker, cuckoo, flycatcher, etc.)— prefers insects, spiders, or worms, but may also eat seeds, nuts, etc.
- ❏ *fruit and seed lover* (sparrow, dove, pigeon, etc.)—prefers fruits and/or seeds, but may also eat insects, spiders, and worms

3 Involving the class. Explain that each kind of bird has a body that helps it find and eat the special kinds of food it needs. Birds that eat seeds and insects need bills that make it easy to pick up tiny things. Often these birds have short bills that work like tweezers. [Let children try to pick up small seeds with tweezers.]

Explain that seed eaters can often spend the winter in very cold areas while insect eaters cannot. Why? [Because insects disappear in very cold weather while seeds remain abundant.]

Have children cut pictures of foods from various magazines and books and paste them in the appropriate sections of the bulletin board.

Extension idea! Create a similar bulletin board using birds of prey (hawks, owls, vultures, etc.) and birds who eat seafood (pelicans, flamingos, cranes, etc.).

Resources: Bird Guides

- ❏ Golden Bird Guides
- ❏ Peterson Bird Guides

Science Sheet Notes

Birds That Hunt, page 140—Use this page to introduce your students to birds of prey. Teach children the major birds-of-prey groups: vultures, hawks, and falcons. Children will be interested to learn that all of these birds hunt during the day. Some eat relatively large animals (rattlesnakes, rabbits, etc.). Many of the birds are very large. The California condor, for example, has a wingspan of 10 feet. [The California condor, unfortunately, is almost extinct.]

We Love Vegetables!, page 141—The majority of birds eat a combination of seeds and insects. The birds on this page, however, prefer a diet of plant foods. This sheet presents an excellent opportunity to study one of America's favorite birds in depth—the turkey. Turkeys are good runners. They eat acorns, fruits, and seeds. Only the male turkey (Tom, by name) gobbles. He gobbles to call his sweethearts home to the harem!

Name _____

Birds That Hunt

Color the birds. Cut out the pictures. Paste each picture onto its matching shape.
[See page 139.]

eagle   owl   hawk   falcon

Name _____

We Love Vegetables

Cut along the dotted lines. Paste the birds next to each other on a long strip of construction paper—from smallest to largest. [See page 139.]

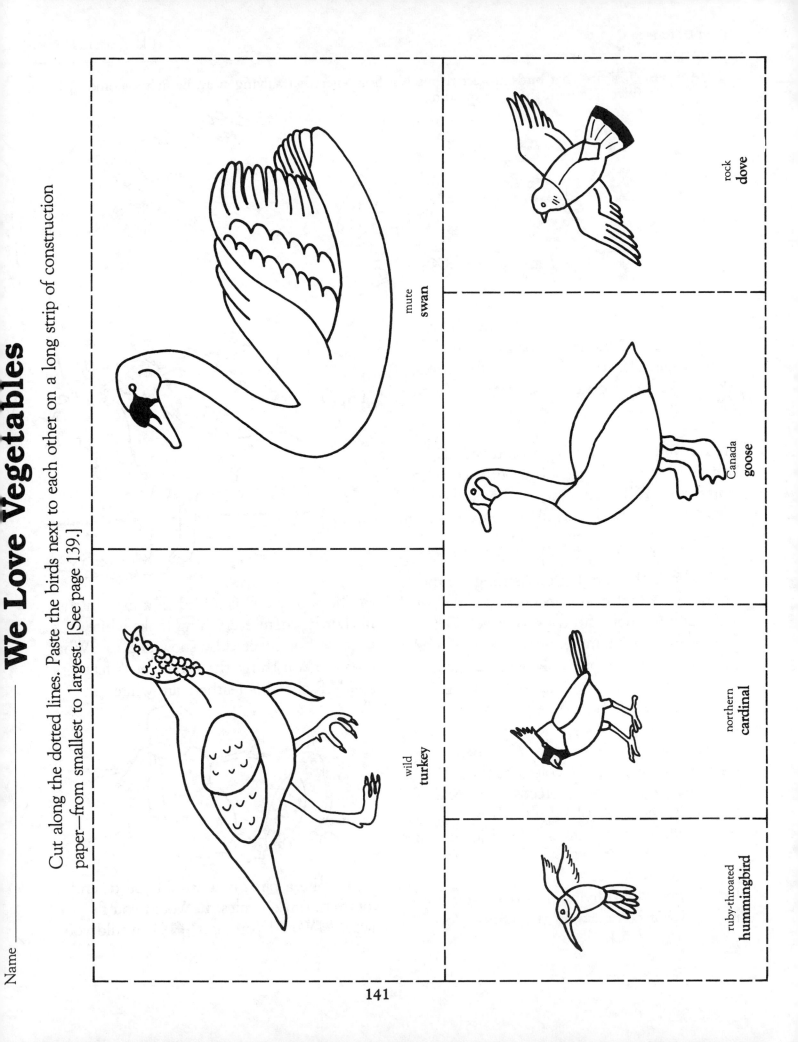

mute
swan

rock
dove

Canada
goose

wild
turkey

northern
cardinal

ruby-throated
hummingbird

Objective: To learn that birds protect themselves from enemies by flying away, by fighting, and by blending with their surroundings.

Flee, Fight, or Hide?

Because most birds are small, they have to defend themselves against bigger animals who would like to eat them. Snakes, foxes, dogs, and many other animals try to catch birds.

If you were a robin, what would you do when a big fox opened his mouth to try to catch you? ■ That's right—you would fly away. Because birds can fly, it's easy for them to get away from their enemies.

Some birds that are big and strong—with sharp claws and beaks and heavy wings—will fight any animal who tries to attack. The bald eagle, for example, weighs as much as 80 pounds—that's probably twice as heavy as you! And the only animal that the eagle is likely to lose a fight to is a person.

Most birds are able to hide from their enemies because of the colors of their feathers. Their colors protect them because they help the birds blend into their surroundings—that makes it hard for enemies to spot them.

If you were a bird living in a dark green jungle, what color would you choose for your feathers? Why?

■ The snowy owl is a bird that lives in the far north where everything looks white because it is covered by snow and ice. What color do you think the snowy owl's feathers are? ■ Right—his feathers are white.

If you were a bird, how would you defend yourself from enemies? ■ Would you fly away? ■ Would you fight? ■ Or would you hide?

142

Vocabulary

camouflage—When an animal's body covering (feathers, hair, scales, etc.) is similar in color to the surroundings that the animal lives in, we say that one of the animal's natural defenses is camouflage.

❑ Jungle & Arctic Camouflage

You need: 2 large sheets of paper (butcher paper works well)
paints and brushes
copies of page 144
crayons, scissors, tape

1 On a large sheet of paper, let the children help you paint a jungle scene that includes an abundance of green trees and vines. On the other large sheet, paint a snowy scene, using primarily white and pale blue paints. Make the trees in this scene gray and lifeless.
2 Give each child a copy of page 144. Have the children color the birds, as indicated, and cut them out.
3 Have each child tape his or her birds onto the painted background that will help the birds hide most easily. As a follow-up to this activity, take the children outside and ask them to try to spot birds in the trees. How are the birds colored? Is it easy or hard to see them?

❑ Feather Plays

You need: a collection of feathers that vary in size and color
materials of various colors (leaves, twigs, dirt, rocks, etc.) displayed in their own boxes

1 **Tray experiments.** Put the feathers and trays of materials on a table. Have children experiment with the feathers by placing them on top of the various materials. Which background material hides each feather best?
2 **I spy!** The day before you play this game, hide 10-15 feathers around the room. [Try to place each feather with a background of similar color.] The next day, tell the children that you've hidden feathers about the classroom in places that make them hard to see. Give awards to children who have the best "eagle" eyes in class.

❑ Hidden Bird Diorama

This activity works well, depending on the ages of the children, with individuals or groups. For a group activity, use one large box for the diorama and make certain that all children choose birds of the same color.
1 Ask children to bring in shoeboxes and toilet tissue rolls a few days before you plan to do this activity.
2 Begin by having each child choose one of the birds from page 144, color it, and cut it out.
3 Discuss the bird's color. Ask the child what background color for the box's interior will help the bird hide best. Have the child paint the inside of the box with an appropriate color.
4 Have children paint the tubes brown. When they're dry, tape strips of green (for summer) or white (for winter) tissue paper to the tubes for foliage. Tape the tube trees inside the box.
5 Have children place their birds in the dioramas. Whose bird is hardest to find?

Science Sheet Notes

Jungle & Arctic Birds, page 144—Use this sheet with the "Jungle & Arctic Camouflage" activity on this page. These cutouts also can be used to make wonderful stick puppets!

Jungle & Arctic Birds

[See page 143.]

The toucan's bill is orange.

yellow

white

black

red

white

gray

The snowy owl is all white except for the eyes, which are yellow.

144

Objective: To learn that birds live where there is adequate food and where they can stay warm.

Where's My Home?

Birds live everywhere in the world. It's easy for them to move around from place to place because most of them can fly. When the weather turns too cold or too hot or when there doesn't seem to be much food around, the birds simply fly to a new place.

Why do you think birds choose to live in a particular place? ■ Usually, birds try to find places where there is plenty of food and where they are safe from enemies. The area that a bird lives in is called a *habitat*. A forest is a habitat for some birds; a jungle is for others. Can you think of any other habitats? (desert, ocean, lake, etc.)

■ Most ducks like to live on ponds or lakes surrounded by forests. They eat seeds, berries, and insects from the forest and plants from the pond. At night, they often float on the water with their heads stuck under their wings so they can sleep.

Most robin red breasts also like to live in forests. But sometimes they live in towns and cities. They search for worms, insects, and seeds to eat during the day. But at night, they perch on tree branches and sleep. The toes on their feet wrap around the branches so they won't fall off even when asleep!

Canada geese like to live way up north during the summer. They swim in rivers and lakes as they search for water grass, seeds, and insects. When the weather starts to turn cold and the plants and insects begin to disappear, the geese gather their families and fly south with other geese—where there is more food. But at the end of winter, they'll fly back to the north.

If you were a bird, would you rather live on land or water? ■ In a jungle or in a snowy place?

duck

robin

Canada goose

145

Vocabulary

habitat—the area where an animal lives. Forests, jungles, oceans, deserts, polar regions, grasslands, and mountains are considered habitats.

☐ The Habitat Game

This game will help children understand this important concept.

1 Ask children if they remember from the story what a habitat is. Explain that a habitat is the area where an animal lives. In its habitat, an animal finds all the things it needs in order to survive, such as food and shelter.

2 Have the children form a circle. Explain that you will name a habitat. Then you'll whisper the name of an animal that lives in that habitat to a child. That child comes into the middle of the circle and pantomimes the animal's movements and mimics its voice for the class. [If children have trouble guessing the name of the animal, give clues.] The child who first guesses the animal in question becomes the next performer. Here are a few habitats and animals to begin:

Habitat	Animal
lake (fresh water)	duck, turtle, frog
ocean	seal, sea gull, octopus
desert	coyote, camel, rattlesnake
arctic	polar bear, walrus
antarctic	emperor penguin, elephant seal
jungle	parrot, monkey, boa constrictor
forest	squirrel, woodpecker, skunk

This is a good game to use in reviewing animals that have been discussed recently.

☐ Funny Bird: A Card Game

1 Preparation. Copy pages 148-149 twice. Color the birds as follows:

- ☐ blue jay—blue in area 1; white in area 2
- ☐ cardinal—red all over
- ☐ robin—gray in area 1; orange in area 2
- ☐ funny bird—your choice
- ☐ flamingo—pink all over
- ☐ duck—brown all over
- ☐ gull—leave white
- ☐ flycatcher—red in area 1; brown in area 2
- ☐ elf owl—brown all over with white streaks on underside
- ☐ roadrunner—blue around eye

For durability, cover the cards with clear plastic adhesive. Cut out cards along the dotted lines.

2 Partner play. [Remove one funny bird card from the deck.] Shuffle the cards together. Deal five cards, facedown, to each player. Put the cards remaining in the deck facedown between the two players.

Each player checks his or her hand to see if there are any matching cards. If so, the players remove those cards and place them faceup on the table.

Then each player, in turn, asks his or her opponent for a card—for example, "the flamingo"—that he or she needs to make a pair with a card already held. [Children may show the card they're trying to match rather than calling out the bird's name.] If the opponent does not have the card, the player must draw one card from the deck. The player who matches the most cards by game's end is the winner. If there's a tie, the player holding the funny bird card is the winner.

3 Solo play. Leave the cards you've prepared in the science center. Children can sort the cards into pairs.

Science Sheet Notes

The Canada Geese, page 147—After children color the pictures and count the Canada geese, ask them to circle the leader and draw a box around the smallest bird.

Funny Bird Cards, pages 148-149—Use these sheets for the Funny Bird game. Once children are familiar with the cards on these pages, have them sort the birds into groups by habitat: *city birds*, *desert birds*, and *water birds*. Funny Bird definitely seems to be a city bird!

Funny Bird Coloring (See directions under Funny Bird: A Card Game)

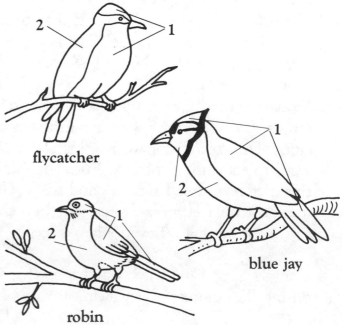

flycatcher

robin

blue jay

The Canada Geese

Color the picture. Count the birds. [See page 146.]

How many geese? _____

Funny Bird Cards

[See page 146.]

bluejay

cardinal

robin

funny bird

flamingo

Funny Bird Cards

[See page 146.]

duck

gull

flycatcher

elf owl

roadrunner

Objective: To learn that birds make nests to keep eggs and chicks safe.

All About Nests

The little mother blue jay perched next to a half-finished nest in a tree. All of a sudden she swooped down to the ground and grabbed a piece of bright red yarn that lay among the leaves. What do you think she was going to do with the yarn? ■Right! She was going to use it in building her nest.

blue jay

Mother birds use many different building materials to make their nests. Most use twigs, grass, and leaves. Some mothers add yarn, string, and other things that catch their eyes as they look for building materials.

What makes all of these things stick together in the nest? ■Well, some birds—such as blue jays and robins—use mud. Hummingbirds use spider webs. Swifts are birds that use the spit from their mouths, which is thick and gummy, to make the grass and twigs in their nests hold together.

Birds build nests because they need a place to lay their eggs. When the eggs hatch, the baby birds need a safe place to live. Mother birds, after all, sometimes leave their babies alone for a short time while looking for food. They need to know their babies are safe at home.

Birds that are good flyers have nests in bushes or trees. Birds that cannot fly or are poor flyers tend to have nests on the ground. Why do you think that is? (Good flyers can get to higher places.)

■In the nest, eggs are usually incubated—which means they are kept warm—by the mother. How does she warm her eggs? ■She sits on them. The heat from her body keeps them warm. If the eggs grow cold, the baby birds inside die.

If you were a baby bird inside an egg, how would you get out of the shell? ■You'd peck a hole with your beak! Then you'd be hatched. When a chicken pecks its way into the world, it can see, it can walk, and it has a warm coat of feathers. It can feed itself within a few hours. But other baby birds, such as hummingbirds, are born blind. They have no feathers and their legs are so weak they cannot stand or walk. These babies—like human babies—need lots of help from their mothers before they're able to take care of themselves.

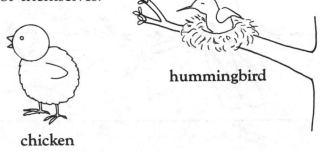

chicken

hummingbird

If you were a baby bird, would you rather be like a chicken or like a hummingbird?

150

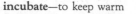

Vocabulary

incubate—to keep warm

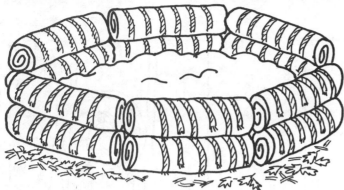

☐ Cozy Nest

Children will enjoy helping you make this nest!

You need: 10-12 paper grocery sacks (or 30 gallon plastic garbage bags)
shredded or crumpled newpapers
masking tape and scissors
string or twine
one or more large blankets
construction paper and crayons
(optional) cardboard, paint, brushes; black, blue, or green yarn and glue

1 Loosely stuff 10-12 bags with newspapers. Roll the stuffed bags into log shapes, as shown, and fasten closed with tape or string.

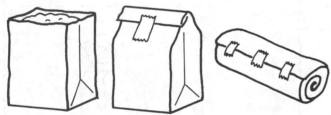

2 Now stack one log on top of another and bind the two together with tape or twine. Make 5-6 of these double logs.
3 In the science center or dramatic play area, put the double logs in a circle and fasten them together with tape. [Note: To make the construction more nest-like, glue small pieces of yarn to the bags.]
4 Place a cozy blanket inside the "nest." If desired, take a walk and collect leaves, sticks, or straw to place on and around the nest.
5 Use the nest as a reading area. Ask the children how it feels to be in a nest? How do the children think a baby bird feels? What would they do if they lived in a nest? How would their lives be different?
6 Give each child a sheet of construction paper and crayons. Help the children write stories about baby birds. Let them illustrate their stories. Display finished stories around the nest. If desired, cut a tree shape out of a large piece of cardboard. Paint it and prop it up near the nest.

☐ Egg Races

1 Draw a chalk line on the floor. Divide children into two teams of equal size. Have each team form a straight line behind the chalk marking.
2 Give the first child in each line an egg and a metal spoon. [For safety, use plastic, candy, or hard-boiled eggs. Let younger children use a cup rather than a spoon.]
3 Stand 10'-12' from the children with the spoons. On your signal, the children race toward you with the eggs balanced on the spoons. If an egg falls off along the way, the child simply picks it up and puts it back on the spoon and continues. Each child must touch you before returning to his or her line—where the spoon and egg are passed to the next child.
4 The first team whose members have all carried the spoon and egg are the winners!

☐ Egg Checklist

✔ Have an egg hunt. Use plastic or candy eggs.
✔ Hold an egg-counting contest to practice math skills.
✔ Color eggs with children to teach primary and secondary colors.
✔ Break open an egg to teach children basic egg parts:
  1. *the shell*—the outside of the egg
  2. *the membrane*—the cellophane-like material that lines the shell
  3. *the albumen*—the egg white
  4. *the yolk*—the yellow center

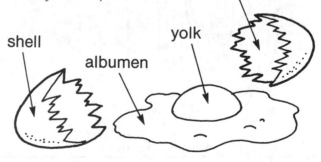

Science Sheet Notes

Hatch Match, page 152—Remind youngsters that birds hatch from eggs. Explain that chicks usually look like their parents, except they are smaller. Then give children this sheet to complete.
All About Nests, page 153—Explain that different kinds of birds build different kinds of nests. The flamingo and duck are water birds that build ground nests. The flamingo's nest is a mound of mud. The duck makes her nest from decaying plants and water-soaked grasses. Eagles use sticks to build their nests (called *aeries*) in the tops of trees or on high cliffs. They decorate their nests with fresh green leaves. Orioles weave hanging nests from grass and twigs.

Hatch Match

Color the pictures. Cut along the dotted lines. Paste the baby birds next to their parents. [See page 151.]

penguin	
ostrich	
woodpecker	
owl	

All About Nests

Color the pictures. Cut out the birds along the dotted lines. Paste each bird on the correct nest. [See page 151.]

eagle

oriole

flamingo

duck

153

Objective: To study the nature and habits of penguins.

Guess Who!

Antarctica is a very cold place where there's ice and snow all year round. It is the home of a bird that cannot fly. This bird waddles when it walks and swims well. Can you guess it's name?

■Right—a penguin! Penguins have thick black feathers over most of their bodies—except for their bellies which have white feathers. Their wings look like flippers and their feet are webbed like a duck's. Do you think these birds can swim? ■Yes! They're wonderful swimmers.

But how can penguins stay warm in a place that's so cold? ■For one thing, they have lots of fat on their bodies. The fat helps keep them warm. They also have very thick feathers that are waterproof. These feathers keep cold water away from the penguins' bodies. It's almost like wearing a raincoat!

Penguins live together in huge groups called *rookeries*. Sometimes, up to one million birds are in one rookery. The bodies of so many birds living together give off lots of heat. That keeps all the birds warmer. Can you imagine what would happen if everyone in our class stood together in one big group? ■Do you think everyone would feel warm?

Guess where penguins hunt for food! ■Right—they go fishing in the ocean. Their favorite seafood is a tiny animal that tastes like shrimp. It's called *krill*. Penguins also dive deep down under the water for squid and fish. Penguins can stay underwater for twenty minutes without coming up for air. How long can you stay underwater?

■On land, penguins can't walk too well. So when they're in a hurry, they just drop down on their bellies and slide across the ice. Almost everything is covered with ice where they live so they do a lot of sliding.

Even though penguins are strong, they still have some enemies. Leopard seals and killer whales love to eat penguins. Penguins have to be very careful to stay together in groups when they go swimming and fishing.

Would you like to live where it always seems like winter?

The Penguin's Enemies

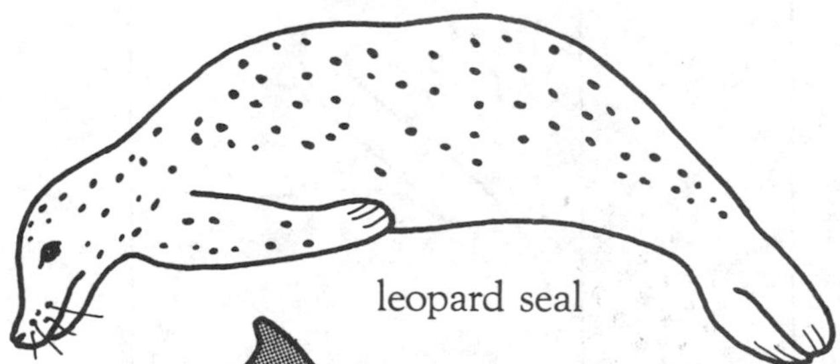

leopard seal

killer whale

154

Penguins on Ice

Vocabulary

rookery—a large group of penguins who live together
krill—a small sea animal that penguins eat; tastes like shrimp

☐ Emperor Penguins: Story and Minibook

Read this story to your class. Then give each child a copy of pages 157-158 to color and cut apart. Have children put the pictures in order and staple them together along the left-hand side of the page.

How Emperor Penguins Grow Up

Emperor penguins are the largest of all penguins. When they are full-grown, they stand four feet tall. Is anyone in class that tall? Each one weighs one hundred pounds. That's probably almost twice as heavy as you are!

When it is autumn in Antarctica, each female penguin lays a single egg on the ice. Then she goes for a two-month long swim. As soon as she leaves, the father takes the egg, lifts it onto his feet, and lets the fat of his belly hang over it to keep it warm. All the fathers in the rookery then huddle in one big group to stay warm. They stay like this for two months—and they don't eat during all this time.

When a chick hatches from an egg, it is fed a thick milky substance that comes from its father's throat. The father sticks his beak into the chick's open mouth and pushes in the food. Within a few days after the chick hatches, the mother comes home to care for it. Then the father leaves to go on a three-week-long hunt for food in the ocean.

After the three weeks have passed, all the fathers return to the mothers and the chicks with food. Everyone has a big meal, and then all the newborn chicks are herded into the center of a circle. The grown-ups stand on the outside of the circle to keep the cold antarctic wind off the chicks and to protect the chicks from enemies.

After six months, the chicks are grown-up enough to take care of themselves.

☐ Penguin Puppets

Make a copy of the penguin on this page for each child. Have the children paste their penguins onto construction paper and cut them out. Paste or tape the cutouts to craft sticks. Have children use the puppets to retell the story.

☐ Penguin Party

1 Dress-up. Have everyone dress up in black and white.
2 Penguin moves. Show children how to walk stiff-legged to mimic the penguin waddle. By keeping their arms straight as they move them, children can also mimic the penguin's use of flippers. Play a penguin version of Simon Says in which each move children make must be penguin-like.
3 Penguin food. Cap off you party with tuna sandwiches!

Science Sheet Notes

Emperor Penguins Minibook, pages 157-158—After children have listened to the story on this page, give them copies of these sheets. Have them color the pages, cut them apart along the dotted lines, and staple them together to make a minibook.

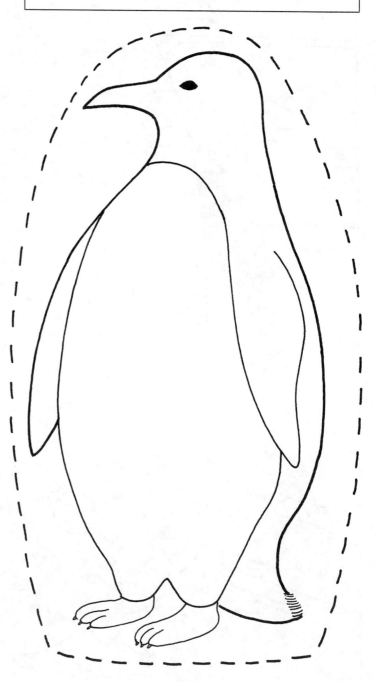

Emperor Penguins Minibook

[See page 156.]

1

My family lives in Antarctica. 2

I cannot fly... 3

but I can swim! 4

Emperor Penguins Minibook

[See page 156.]

I eat krill and fish.　⑤

Before I hatched, daddy put my egg
on his feet to keep me warm.　⑥

When I hatched,
mommy took care of me.　⑦ Daddy brought us food from the ocean. ⑧

Mammals

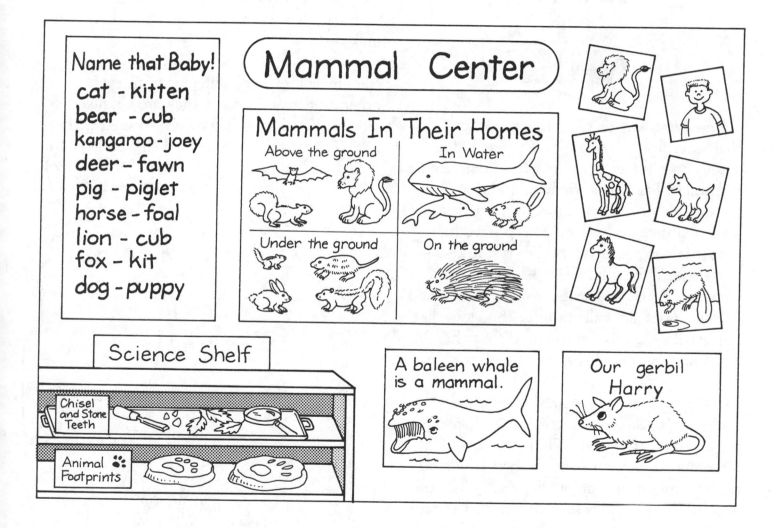

Name that Baby!
cat - kitten
bear - cub
kangaroo - joey
deer - fawn
pig - piglet
horse - foal
lion - cub
fox - kit
dog - puppy

Mammal Center

Mammals In Their Homes

Above the ground

In Water

Under the ground

On the ground

Science Shelf

Chisel and Stone Teeth

Animal Footprints

A baleen whale is a mammal.

Our gerbil Harry

Objective: To learn that mammals have hair and that they provide milk for their young.

A Hairy Coat and Lots of Milk

The easiest way to tell a mammal from all the other animals is to see if it has hair. That's because *all* mammals have hair. Some mammals, like bears, rabbits, and dogs have lots of soft, thick hair called fur. Fur keeps a mammal nice and warm. Sheep have hair too. It is curly and twisty. Do you know what sheep's hair is called? ■ That's right, it's wool. Porcupine hairs are long, hard, and prickly. They are called quills; they look like big needles. Quills are so sharp that they can hurt an animal that gets stuck with one.

Most mammals have hair all over their bodies, but some mammals don't. Take a look around the room. There are lots of mammals here with hair on their heads but not too much hair anywhere else. What do you think we call these mammals? ■ That's right! They're people. Another term for people is *human beings*. Can you say "human beings"? Human beings are mammals too; our hair covers only part of our bodies.

Mammals not only have hair—they are the only animals that have milk for their babies to drink. Have you ever seen a mother dog nursing her puppies? ■ The puppies suck milk from large glands under her belly called breasts. Human babies nurse from their mothers' breasts too. Have you ever seen a mommy nursing her baby? ■ Some mammal mothers, like cows, have so much milk that their calves don't need it all. The farmer milks the cows so people can drink their milk too.

Mammals look very different from each other, but in some ways they are all alike. Do you know how? [They are covered with hair. They provide milk for their young.]

160

Mammals

cow

rabbit

porcupine

sheep

child

dog

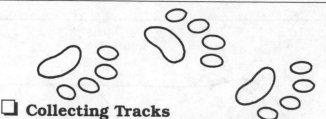

Vocabulary

breast—a gland found in female mammals that gives milk
nurse—to feed milk to a baby from a mother's breasts
quills—the hollow, sharp spines of a porcupine or hedgehog

❑ Mammal Hair Questionnaire

Bring in samples of different kinds of mammal hair: fur, hide with hair in place, and wool. Place the samples at the science center and label them. Let children touch each sample. Ask some of the following questions:

1 Which kind of hair keeps the mammal warmest? (thick fur)
2 Which kind of hair can we get without hurting the mammal? (wool)
3 How do you think we get fur or hide from a mammal? [The mammal must be killed first.]
4 Since we can get most of the materials for our clothes from plants (cotton, linen), do you think we should kill mammals for their fur?

❑ Zoo Music

1 Cut out pictures of each animal mentioned in the song below: kangaroo, lion, elephant, bear, giraffe, monkey. You can use pictures on this page and on pages 163, 169, and 176. Duplicate pictures enough times so that each child can have one.
2 Teach children the song, to the tune of "Row, Row, Row Your Boat." Ask children to hold up their pictures only when their animal's name is mentioned in the song.

We're going on a trip today,
We'll see a kangaroo,
We'll hear the lion's great big roar,
We'll meet you at the zoo.

Elephants will swing their trunks,
Bears will play and run,
Giraffes will hold their heads up high,
And monkeys will have fun.

❑ Neighborhood Mammals

Take a walk in the neighborhood of your school. You're sure to find a variety of four-legged furry friends! You will probably see other kinds of animals too. Help children recognize those with hair (fur, hide, wool) and four legs. When you return to the classroom, have children help you create a chart of mammals you saw and places you saw them. Bring in pictures of the mammals to add to the chart. [As an alternative, visit a pet shop or a zoo.]

❑ Collecting Tracks

You can tell a lot about a mammal by looking at its footprints—what kind of mammal it is; how big it is. [Some collectors can even tell how fast a mammal moves by looking at its footprints.] If you're lucky, you can find a clear print in mud. If not, have a child get an impression in clay of his or her pet dog or cat. You may also wish to have children make impressions of their own footprints. Here's what to do:

You need: paintbrush
bottomless, topless tin can (wide as possible)
plaster of Paris
water

1 Brush off the footprint to be sure it is free of loose debris.
2 Place the can over the footprint and press down so the can is firmly in place. [If you need to cover a larger area than the can, round a long strip of stiff plastic or metal into a band.]
3 Follow the directions for mixing on the plaster of Paris package. The mixture should form a thick cream.
4 Pour a one-inch layer of plaster of Paris mixture into the can and let it dry. (about one hour)
5 Remove the cast from the can.
6 Have children observe and discuss the way the footprint looks.
7 If you can get both cat and dog footprints, compare them. Display them in the science center.

step 4   step 6

❑ Mammal Checklist

✔ Match the hair. From a big box of fur and wool samples, let children find matching pairs.
✔ Make a silly mammal hair collage. Trace the shape of an animal onto oaktag. Ask children to glue different types of hair on it. Name your animal.
✔ Read Bill Peet's *The Wing-Ding-Dilly*, about an animal who isn't happy as himself and is turned into six different kinds of animals! Make your own Wing-Ding-Dilly.

Science Sheet Notes

Mammal Friends, page 163—Use this sheet after children have listened to the story on page 160. This sheet is also an excellent follow-up for the activities on this page.

Name _____

Mammal Friends

Circle the mammals in each row. Color them. [See page 162.]

Objective: To learn that a mammal's teeth influences its choice of food.

Let's See Your Teeth

Mammals eat many different kinds of foods. You can tell what a mammal eats by looking at its teeth. A lion has great big pointed teeth in the front of its mouth. Have you ever seen them? ■ They are good for tearing meat apart. It also has teeth in its cheeks that work like scissors. These teeth cut and chew the meat. Mammals like lions, tigers, and wolves are meat-eaters. They eat other animals that they catch. They are hunters.

Other mammals, like rabbits, are plant-eaters. Have you ever seen rabbits' teeth? ■ A rabbit has two long, flat front teeth. They are good for biting pieces of wood and for chopping leaves and seeds. Rabbits also have strong back teeth for grinding wood and leaves into tiny little pieces. A rabbit's teeth never stop growing, but they never get too long. Do you know why? ■ It's because the teeth get worn down by the food the rabbit eats.

Some mammals are insect-eaters. Have you ever seen a mammal called an anteater? ■ What do you think it eats? ■ (ants) It has no teeth at all. It uses its sharp claws to tear apart nests of ants. Then it pokes out its long, sticky tongue to capture the ants.

And what about people? We are mammals too. Feel your teeth with your tongue. We have sharp teeth for eating meat, flat teeth for gnawing plants, and bumpy back teeth for chewing and grinding. We can eat all kinds of foods. What other animals can eat all kinds of foods? (dogs, bears, etc.)

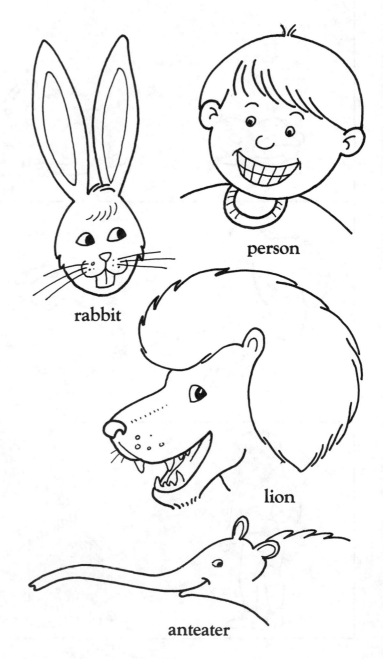

person

rabbit

lion

anteater

164

Vocabulary

gnaw—to bite again and again

chisel—a metal tool with a sharp edge at the end of a blade used to cut wood, stone, or metal

baleen whale—a kind a whale with strainer-like plates instead of teeth

☐ Knife and Scissor Teeth

Give children a concrete idea of how a meat-eating mammal eats. Try the experiment below.

You need: small tender piece of meat
plate
2 sharp knives
sharp scissors

1 Place the meat on the plate. Explain that meat-eating mammals can eat food similar to this.

2 Show children the picture of the fox's teeth on page 166. Ask them what the two pointed front teeth look like. (curved knives)

3 Have children find their own canines (eye teeth) and feel how sharp they are.

4 Use the knives to cut the meat apart as a fox would tear it with its teeth.

5 Explain that the fox's back teeth work like scissors to cut and chew the meat. Have children use their tongues to feel the ridges of their own back teeth. Cut the meat (already cut with knives) with the scissors to show how a fox cuts and chews. Cut until the meat is in small pieces.

6 Show children the way the meat looks before it is ready to be swallowed.

☐ Chisel and Stones Teeth

To help children understand what kinds of teeth a plant-eating mammal has, have children assist you with the demonstration below.

You need: chisel
small twigs and leaves
wooden board
2 flat stones
mirror

1 Show children the illustration of the beaver's front teeth on this page. Then hold up the chisel. Ask children to notice the similarity between the illustration and the chisel. [Both have sharp, flat edges.]

2 Place the twigs and leaves on the wooden board, and use the chisel to cut them. Explain that teeth like chisels are good for gnawing through wood and seeds.

3 Show children the two flat stones and explain that the stones work the way a plant-eater's back teeth work.

4 Place some leaves (already chisel-cut) between the two stones and have children help grind them. Have children notice the way the leaves look when they are ready to be swallowed.

5 Then have children feel the bottom of their own teeth. Let them look at their front teeth in a mirror. Ask: Do your front teeth look and feel like a chisel? (yes) What kinds of food do your front teeth help you eat? (vegetables and other foods that are gnawed)

☐ Strainers and Brushes

To help children understand how a baleen whale eats, have them assist you with the demonstration below.

You need: small can flaked fish
1 quart water
2 large plastic containers (one wider-mouthed than the other)
wire strainer or straw brush

1 Enlarge the illustration of the baleen whale's head on this page. Show it to the children and explain that some whales have no teeth; instead they have brushlike strainers (baleen plates) in their mouths. Baleen whales suck large quantities of water and krill (small sea creatures) into their mouths. Then they catch the krill with their "strainers" as they squeeze the water out of their mouths.

2 Let a child place the flaked fish and water in the wider-mouthed container. Tell children to pretend that this container is holding some ocean water and krill. Then pour this mixture into the second container. Have children pretend that this container is the baleen whale sucking in the ocean water and the krill. If you wish, decorate the second container with construction paper to look like a baleen whale with its mouth open.

3 Finally, pour the water and krill mixture back into the first container, only this time let a child hold the wire strainer or straw brush over the lip of the second container (whale's mouth).

4 Have children notice all the fish that is captured in the strainer. Let children take turns capturing food.

Science Sheet Notes

A Foxy Smile, page 166—Have each child make a smiling fox puppet that shows its teeth! Children will enjoy pretending to be foxes and sharing their adventures with each other. They can move the head up and down to see the fox's teeth and make it "talk."

You need: crayons
scissors
paste
copies of fox cutouts
oaktag
brass fasteners

1 Have children color and cut out their fox cutouts.

2 Mount the pieces on oaktag and cut out again. Laminate for extra durability.

3 Punch a hole on each piece as indicated by the large dots. Use a brass fastener to attach the pieces. The upper jaw is placed over the lower jaw. [See illustration.]

A Foxy Smile

[See instruction on page 165.]

Objective: To learn that mammals defend themselves by using camouflage, by fighting, by running away, and in the case of people, by talking things out.

Mammals— Watch Out!

Most mammals have enemies that want to catch and eat them. They have to protect themselves—but how? ■ Many mammals are lucky enough to be the same colors as the places they live in. When they stand very still, their enemies can hardly see them. They look like part of their surroundings. This is called *camouflage*.

A zebra has black stripes that make it look like the dark trees it stands next to. A leopard has spots that look like brown shadows in the forest. And in icy cold places, polar bears are as white as the snow. Have you ever heard of an animal with green hair? ■ A mammal called a sloth lives in the green jungles of South America. The sloth's greenish-grey hair makes it look like the green leaves on the trees. Its hair looks green because many tiny green plants stick to the sloth's fur. Do you think the sloth has good camouflage?

■ If a mammal can't hide from its enemies, it can stay and fight. Horses can kick enemies with their strong legs. Goats can stab enemies with their sharp horns. And kangaroos can hit enemies with their strong hind legs or tear their enemy's skin with their sharp claws. Porcupines hurt their enemies with their sharp needlelike quills. If a quill gets into an animal's eye, the animal can be blinded. And skunks get rid of enemies with their terrible smell. Who would want to get near a mammal that smells so bad?

A small mammal has lots of trouble protecting itself. It would probably lose a fight with a bigger enemy, so it must run away. Chipmunks dive into underground homes where their enemies can't reach them. Squirrels scurry up the sides of trees, and beavers dive into the water.

But how do people, the smartest mammals of all, defend themselves? ■ We use our words to try to talk things out, of course. If we have to, we can yell very loudly to tell others we're in trouble; we can run, drive, or ride away very fast; we can stand very still and hide where we cannot be seen; or we can stay and fight. People have many ways of defending themselves!

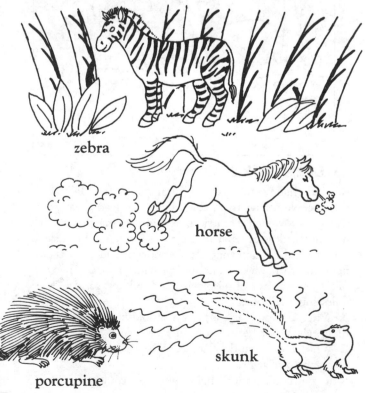

zebra

horse

porcupine

skunk

167

Vocabulary

camouflage—When an animal's body covering (feathers, hair, scales, etc.) is similar in color to the surroundings that the animal lives in, we say that one of the animal's natural defenses is camouflage.

quills—the hollow, sharp spines of a porcupine or hedgehog

☐ Hidden Pictures

You need: 12″×18″ construction paper
brown, tan, and green crayons
scissors

1 Talk about the word *camouflage*. Explain that many kinds of mammals can blend in with their surroundings so they can hide.
2 On a sheet of construction paper, have each child draw a forest or jungle, using different shades of brown, tan, and green.
3 On another sheet of paper have each child draw a mammal, using the same colors. [You may wish to trace some of the mammals on page 169 for the children. You can enlarge the pictures with an opaque projector.]
4 Help children cut out the animals. Then cut a long horizontal slit in each child's picture, as shown on this page. [For durability, paste each child's picture on top of another sheet of construction paper before making the slit.]
5 Insert the lower part of the mammal through the slit so only the upper part of the body shows. Children can slide their "hidden" mammals along the slits.

☐ Let's Talk It Over

Remind children that people are mammals too. Talk about ways people defend themselves. [This can lead to very thought-provoking discussion, as many young children have unrealistic ideas of what to do in case they need to defend themselves.] Explain that people not only hide, but they can fight and run away. In fact, people can do more—they can talk their way out of problems! Ask children some of the following questions:
1 When do you think a person should fight? run away? hide? talk his or her way out of a problem?
2 What would you do if someone bigger and stronger than you wanted to fight?
3 If you didn't want to fight, what else could you do?

☐ *Aesop's Fables*

Aesop's Fables includes some wonderful stories that show how, among other things, different animals defend themselves, especially by trickery. Read some of these fables to your class: "The Cat and the Fox," "A Wolf in Sheep's Clothing," and "The Cat and the Mice."

☐ Mammal Grab Bag

Talk about the ways mammals defend themselves: hiding, fighting, running away. Then, on index cards, write the names and tape pictures of mammals you have talked about in class. Place the cards inside a large paper bag, and have each child, in turn, select one (without looking inside the bag). The child then tells the class which way the mammal protects itself from an enemy. [Help children as needed. For example, you might say, "Look at the lion's sharp teeth. See its strong claws. It looks very, very strong. Do you think it would run away? How do you think it would defend itself?"] If you wish, reward each child with an mammal sticker. Some mammals you might include are:

Hide	Fight	Run Away
leopard: spots	cat: sharp claws	horses
zebra: stripes	sheep: sharp horns	zebras
giraffe: spots	kangaroo: strong legs	cheetah
fawn: spots	horses: strong legs	rabbit
lion: sandy color	donkey: strong legs	deer
polar bear: white color	lion: strong teeth	
sloth: greenish color	woodchuck: strong teeth	

Science Sheet Notes

White as the Snow, page 169—Before completing their science sheets, explain to children that the fur of some mammals of the Far North turns white during the winter. These animals can hide from their enemies by blending in with the snow. After children have completed their science sheets, have them cut out the white animals and mount them on sheets of white construction paper. Be sure children cut inside the outlines, so the outlines do not show on the white construction paper background. Discuss how difficult it would be to find a white mammal on the white snow. If appropriate, label the animals. (The white mammals on the worksheet are the Arctic fox, Arctic hare, Arctic wolf, and polar bear.)

Name _____

White as the Snow

In each picture, circle two mammals that are as white as the snow. Color the other mammals.
[See page 168.]

Objective: To learn that mammals can live in all parts of the world.

A Home for a Mammal

Mammals live just about everywhere. They live *above* the ground, *on* the ground, and *under* the ground. They live in hot places and in cold places. They live in wet places and in dry places. Some mammals even live in the water.

Many mammals live in the forest. Squirrels live above the ground in trees. They build round nests out of leaves and twigs in the treetops. That's a nice, comfortable place for a squirrel family. Raccoons live in tree trunks too. They look for holes in trees and line the holes with soft grass and moss. Then they move in.

Porcupines live on the forest floor. When it gets cold, they move into small caves or the stumps of old trees. They don't do anything to make their homes safe. Why do you think that is so? [Their quills will keep most enemies away. They don't need a well-protected home.]

■Chipmunks dig underground homes with lots of rooms. Each room is used for something different. Some rooms are for sleeping, others are for storing food, and a few are for piling garbage during the winter.

Beavers make their homes in water. They build round houses of twigs, grass, and mud. The houses sit in the middle of a forest stream. Each house has a little hole at the top. Why do you think a beaver needs this hole? [The hole is for breathing air.]

Where else do mammals live? ■Elephants and zebras live in very hot places. Polar bears and Arctic foxes live in cold places filled with snow and ice. Camels and lions live in dry places that have few trees. And monkeys live in wet jungles where it rains a lot. Do you know where whales and dolphins live? ■That's right! They live in the ocean. Because they are mammals, they must swim to the surface of the water to breathe air. Instead of a nose, they have a blowhole on top of their heads. Have you ever seen a whale or dolphin shoot a fountain of water mist from its blowhole into the air? ■When you see this fountain, it means the animal is breathing out the old air just before taking in fresh air.

170

Vocabulary

habitat—a place where animals and plants naturally live and grow
hibernate—to spend a period of time in an inactive state with a lower body temperature
blowhole—the hole on top of a whale's or dolphin's head through which it breathes

☐ "Mammal Homes" Bulletin Board

You need: 5 different colors of construction paper
dark marker
photographs or drawings of animal homes

1 Back the bulletin board with light-colored construction paper.
2 Place the other four colors of construction paper across the board, as shown below.
3 Use the marker to write the title, *Mammals in Their Homes*, across the top of the display. Then label the four sheets as follows: *Above the Ground, On the Ground, Under the Ground,* and *In the Water.*
4 Have children draw or bring in pictures of mammals in their homes. Place each illustration in the correct place on the bulletin board. Here are some mammal suggestions:

☐ *Above the Ground*—Squirrels build leafy homes called dreys in the forks of trees. Bats hang from treetops and cave shelves. Lions sometimes sleep in low trees, although they do not build homes.
☐ *On the Ground*—Porcupines live inside hollow tree stumps, niches in rocks, or small caves. Most large mammals live on the ground, although they do not build homes.
☐ *Under the Ground*—Woodchucks, moles, chipmunks, skunks, and gophers live in holes under the ground. Woodchucks build several tunnels and rooms in their burrows.
☐ *In the Water*—Beavers build round, twiggy lodges in ponds that they create by damming forest streams. The upper portion of the lodge is above water so the beaver can breathe. Whales, dolphins and manatees (sea cows) live in the ocean, but they do not build homes.

Mammals In Their Homes

Above The Ground	On The Ground	Under The Ground	In The Water

☐ Habitat Set

Do you need a home for your class pet? You can purchase an attractive, sturdy home for hamsters, gerbils, or other small mammals from Carolina Biological Supply Company, 2700 York Road, Burlington, North Carolina 27215-3398. This habitat set includes a plastic cage, water bottle, exercise wheel, and a sky pet house.

☐ Homes for Hibernation

Explain that some mammals build homes only for the winter when they hibernate. If you have already introduced the concept of hibernation in the amphibian and reptile sections, review it here. [See pages 68 and 94.] Explain that a mammal is another kind of animal that hibernates. If you are introducing the concept for the first time, bring in pictures to show sleeping mammals in their homes. [A woodchuck is a true hibernating mammal. Most mammals like bears, skunks, moles, and raccoons sleep for only part of the winter.]

☐ Guess Who I Am? Checklist

Play a classroom game in which you pretend to be different mammals. Describe yourself and your habitat. Ask children to guess who you are. Here are some suggestions:

✔I am a big furry mammal. I sometimes live in a cave. I sleep there for part of the winter. Who am I? (a bear)
✔I am a mammal that lives in the ocean. I swim above the water to breathe. I blow warm steam from my blowhole. Who am I? (a whale or a dolphin)
✔I am a mammal that lives in the jungle. My home is above the ground, where I can swing from tree to tree. Who am I? (a monkey)
✔I am a flying mammal. I like to hunt for food at night. I can hang upsidedown in trees. Who am I? (a bat)

Science Sheet Notes

Who Am I?, page 172—Remind children that mammals can live almost anywhere. Then give them this science sheet to complete. After they have discovered the camel, explain that its long legs keep it high above the hot air near the sand. Its heavy eyelids keep the sand out if its eyes. It can travel for a long time without a drink of water.

Mammal Homes, page 173—If appropriate, have each child glue the matching halves onto a large sheet of paper. Write the title *Mammal Homes* at the top. You can also have children identify and write each mammal's name beneath its picture (squirrel, beaver, chipmunk, raccoon). Have children take home their science projects.

Name _____

Who Am I?

I am a mammal. I live on the hot dry desert. I have long legs and a hump on my back. Who am I?   Connect the dots from A to Z. Color the picture.   [See page 171.]

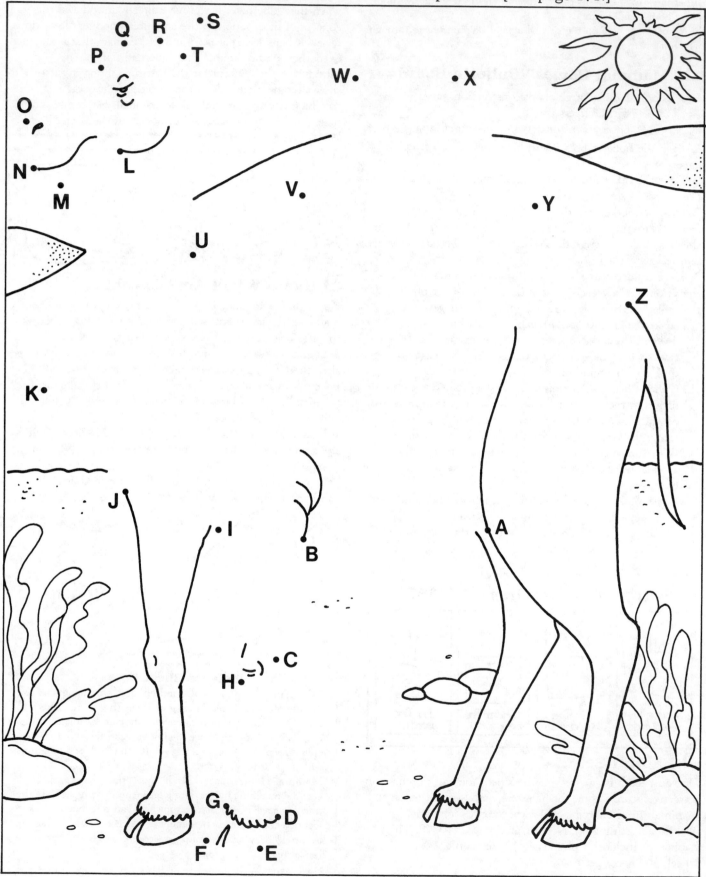

172

Name _____

Mammal Homes

Color the pictures. Cut them apart. Match each mammal to its home. [See page 171.]

Objective: To learn that mammals grow in their mothers' bodies, are born alive, and drink their mothers' milk.

How Do Baby Mammals Grow?

A baby mammal grows inside its mother's body until it is ready to be born. It is very comfortable and warm there. At first the baby mammal is very tiny. As it grows, it starts to look like its mother and father. When a baby is growing inside a mother mammal, we say the mother is pregnant.

Have you ever seen a pregnant woman?
■ Have you ever seen a pregnant cat or dog?
■ The mother's body bulges out to make room for the baby growing inside. Some baby mammals grow in their mother's body for a long time. A baby human grows in its mother's body for nine months. A baby elephant grows in its mother's body for almost two years. Other mammals, such as mice, grow in their mothers' bodies for a very short time—only a few weeks.

When the baby is ready to live in the outside world, it passes through an opening in its mother's body. Then it is born. But the newborn mammal is not ready to find its own food. It has to drink milk from its mother's breasts. Some baby mammals can do very little when they are born. A newborn mouse cannot see or hear. A newborn kangaroo is as small as a quarter. It needs to live in a pocket, called a pouch, on its mother's belly for several months. A baby human cannot walk, talk, get its own food, or even turn over. What else can't a newborn baby human do?

■ There are some newborn mammals, though, that can take care of themselves right away. Newborn cows can stand up and nurse from their mothers the same day they are born. Horses can run with the herd very soon after they are born. What could you do right away when you were born? [You could cry, suck, breathe, move your arms and legs, etc.]

Vocabulary

pregnant—having one or more unborn young developing in a female mammal's body

nurse—to feed milk to a baby from a mother's breasts

marsupial—a kind of mammal. The female has a pouch in which she carries her young.

pouch—a pocketlike part on the outside of a marsupial's body, used to carry its baby

human—having to do with people; men, women, and children

❑ Name the Baby

Ask children what we call a baby dog? (puppy) baby cat? (kitten) Explain that different mammal babies are called by different names. Bring in lots of pictures of mammal babies from library books. Give the name of each baby. Create a chart that is pictorial, for younger children, or written, for older children. Some baby mammals to include are:

bear (cub)	seal (pup)
cow (calf)	horse (foal)
buffalo (calf)	fox (kit)
pig (piglet)	kangaroo (joey)
deer (fawn)	lion (cub)

❑ "Newborn Babies" Bulletin Board

Remind children that we are mammals too, sometimes called *humans*. Hold a discussion about the way a newborn baby looks and what a newborn can do. Ask:

1 When you were a newborn baby, did you look something like your parents? [Yes, you already had a similar-shaped face, similar features, similar coloring, two arms, two legs, etc.]

2 Did you look like any other mammal? [No, each mammal looks like its own kind.]

3 What could you do? (not very much—cry, suck, drink milk, move your arms and legs, sleep)

4 Could you sit, stand, walk, talk? [No.]

Have children bring in photographs of themselves as infants. Create a bulletin board called "Newborn Babies" and display the photographs. If appropriate, write simple captions telling what each baby is doing and what it needs from its mother.

❑ Baby in the Pouch

1 Tell children about some of the unusual mammals of Australia: kangaroos, koalas, and opossums. [If appropriate, introduce the term *marsupial*.] These mammals give birth to very tiny babies—some are only the size of a penny. Explain that once a baby kangaroo, koala, or opossum is born, it crawls into a pocket, called a pouch, on its mother's stomach. While in the pouch, it drinks its mother's milk and grows much bigger and stronger. Some of these babies live in their mothers' pouches for three to six months. [Children will be interested in the fact that opossums are the only mammals with pouches that are native to North America.]

2 Give each child a copy of page 177 to color and cut out.

3 Paste each picture onto oaktag and cut out again.

4 Have children cut a slit along the dotted line on the mother kangaroo and then place the baby in the pouch to move up and down. Be sure to cut around the baby's paws so the paws hook over the mother's pouch.

kangaroo   koala   opossum

❑ Kangaroo Hop

For added fun, have children pretend they are kangaroos. Show them how to hold their hands in front of them and hop. You can even hold a class kangaroo-hopping contest!

❑ Then and Now Display

Create this display to show how much more children can do now than when they were infants. Have each child bring in two photographs—one of them as an infant and one of them as they look now. Post the photographs side by side. Have children tell what they were doing in each picture.

Science Sheet Notes

Mammal Babies, page 176—After they complete the science sheet, have older children write the name of each baby animal next to its picture. (deer—fawn, bear—cub, kangaroo—joey, human—infant.)

Baby in the Pouch, page 177—Use the directions in the "Baby in the Pouch" activity on this page to help children make this piece of art.

Name _____

Mammal Babies

Color the pictures of baby mammals. Cut them out and paste each baby next to its mother. [See page 175.]

deer

bear

kangaroo

human

Name _____

Baby in the Pouch

[See instructions on page 175.]

Objective: To learn the physical characteristics of the cottontail rabbit.

Cottontail Rabbits

Which mammal has long ears, soft fur, whiskers, and hops? ■Did you guess a rabbit? ■Many rabbits, such as the cottontail rabbit, live in the woods. Every spring and summer baby rabbits are born. They are born underground in cozy homes called burrows. Their mother nurses them with warm milk from her breasts. She protects them from enemies like wolves, big birds, bobcats, and dogs. The baby rabbits can't do anything for themselves. They are completely helpless. They have no fur. They can't even see.

In only a few weeks, the bunnies grow soft brown fur and fluffy white tails that look like cotton. They can see, and they can find their own food. Their mother lets them leave the burrow. Then they eat grass, leaves, seeds and tree bark. But they don't look for their food during the day. Instead they find food at night. Do you know why? [The darkness protects them from enemies that are bigger than they are.]

■Cottontail rabbits have very long ears— the better to hear their enemies with. They also have strong legs so they can hop away quickly if they need to. Their eyes bulge out so they can see over their shoulders without turning around. Then they can see anything moving around behind them. Even their whiskers help them. A cottontail rabbit's whiskers are like an extra pair of hands. A rabbit uses its whiskers to feel many of the things around it.

Rabbits make good pets. Tame rabbits are very playful and do not bite. If you keep a rabbit in a clean, comfortable hutch with fresh straw or hay to lie on and leaves and seeds to eat, it will be a very happy pet. Would you like to have a bunny?

Cottontail Rabbit

Vocabulary
hutch—a house for rabbits or other small animals
burrow—a hole dug in the ground by an animal, for a home

❑ Rabbits and Fox Finger Play

Explain to children that rabbits can escape their enemy the fox by hopping away quickly. Teach children the finger play below. Then have them color and cut out the rabbit and fox finger puppets on page 184. Help them fasten the bands with glue or tape to fit on their fingers. Each child wears the rabbit finger puppets on one hand, and the fox finger puppet on the index finger of the other hand. As children say the finger play, they perform the movements indicated.

Here comes the fox, (Hold up rabbit finger puppets.
His mouth open wide.   Wiggle fox finger puppet and move
                         it closer to rabbits.)

What can we do? (Wiggle rabbit finger puppets.)
Quick, let's all hide. (Place hand with rabbit finger
                        puppets behind back.)

Now, where's the fox? (Wiggle fox finger puppet.)
He's gone far away. (Place hand with fox finger puppet
                       behind back.)

Let's all hop out, (Hold up rabbit finger puppets.
                      Wiggle them.)

It's soon time for play. (Move hand up and down.)

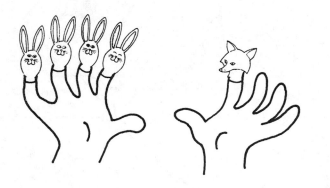

❑ Foxes and Bunnies

1 Have children stand in a large open area. Select one child to be the bunny. The others are the foxes. The bunny stands at one end of the area and the foxes at the other. When the bunny turns away from the foxes and says "Try and catch me," the foxes walk toward the bunny. They must stop, though, before the bunny turns around. If the bunny turns around and finds a fox moving, that child is out of the game and must sit down. The fox that tags the bunny is the next to be the bunny.

2 Make bunny ears for the child selected to be "bunny." From pink construction paper, cut a 2″×2″ band and two bunny-shaped ears. Staple the band to fit a child's head. Staple the ears in place as shown below.

❑ Rabbits Make Good Pets

1 If at all possible, keep a rabbit as a class pet. Provide a hutch, with fresh straw or hay to lie on. Keep the hutch in a cool place, where it does not get sunshine all day long. Feed the rabbit lettuce leaves, carrots, or rabbit food from a pet store. Provide water. Let children take turns caring for it. Children can learn first-hand what a rabbit looks like, how it feels, and what its habits are. [If you cannot keep a class rabbit, perhaps a child could bring in his or hers for the day, or you could visit a pet store.]

2 Even if you don't keep a rabbit, talk about pet care. List ideas and have children draw pictures on an experience chart. Here are some ideas:

A rabbit is a mammal pet.
A rabbit eats plant food.
A rabbit needs water.
A rabbit needs exercise.
Be gentle with a rabbit.
Give a rabbit a clean, safe home.

Science Sheet Notes

Hidden Bunnies, page 181—This science sheet can be completed before you read the story on page 178 or as a culminating activity for this section of the book.

Bunny Book, pages 182-183—After reading "Cottontail Rabbits," have children make this minibook. Children color the pictures, cut them apart, put the pages in order, and staple them together.

Rabbits and Fox, page 184—Use this science sheet for the "Rabbits and Fox Finger Play" described on this page (180).

Name _____

Hidden Bunnies

Circle the bunnies hiding in the picture.

[See page 180.]

Bunny Book

[See page 180.]

When they are born, they have no fur. They cannot see.

③

Cottontail bunnies soon grow soft fur and fluffy white tails.

⑤

My Bunny Book

Name _____

①

Their strong legs help them run fast.

⑧

182

Bunny Book

[See page 180.]

Their long ears help them hear enemies. ⑦

Mother rabbit feeds her babies milk. She protects them from enemies. ④

Cottontail rabbits are born in a burrow underground. ②

The bunnies find their own food. They eat tree bark and plants. ⑥

Name _____

Rabbits and Fox

Color the finger puppets. Cut them out. Tape them to fit your fingers. [See page 180.]

Recommended Books and Animal Shapes

Recommended Books

Here's a list of some of our favorite books about animals.

All About Animals

Barrett, Judi. *Animals should definitely not act like people*

Barrett, Judi. *Animals should definitely not wear clothing*

Barton, Byron. *Buzz, Buzz, Buzz*

Cerf, Bennet. *Book of Animal Riddles*

Kellogg, Steven. *Can I Keep Him?*

Lionni, Leo. *Inch by Inch*

Shapp, Martha and Charles. *Let's Find Out About Animals*

Waber, Bernard. *You Look Ridiculous Said the Rhinoceros to the Hippopotamus*

Insects

Brinkloe, Julie. *Fireflies!*

Carle, Eric. *The Very Hungry Caterpillar*

Conklin, Gladys. *I Like Caterpillars*

Conklin, Gladys. *We Like Bugs*

Hawes, Judy. *Bees & Beelines*

Hawes, Judy. *Fireflies in the Night*

McClung, Robert M. *Green Darner: The Story of a Dragonfly*

Podendorf, Illa. *Insects* (The New True Books)

Selsam, Millicent. *Where Do They Go? Insects in Winter*

Selsam, Millicent and Joyce Hunt. *A First Look at Insects*

Selsam, Millicent and Ronald Goor. *Backyard Insects*

Spiders

Adrian, Mary. *Garden Spider*

Brinekloe, Julie. *The Spider Web*

Carle, Eric. *The Very Busy Spider*

Cullen, Esther. *An Introduction to Australian Spiders*

Goldin, Augusta. *Spider Silk*

McDermott, Gerald. *Anansi the Spider: A Tale from the Ashanti*

McNulty, Faith. *The Lady & the Spider*

Reidman, Sara. *Spiders*

Amphibians

Chenery, Janet. *Toad Hunt*

Cole, Joanna. *A Frog's Body*

Flack, Marjorie. *Tim Tadpole and the Great Bullfrog*

Hawes, Judy. *What I Like about Toads*

Hawes, Judy. *Why Frogs Are Wet*

Kalan, Robert. *Jump, Frog, Jump!*

Kellogg, Steven. *The Mysterious Tadpole*

Kent, Jack. *The Caterpillar & the Polliwog*

Lobel, Arnold. *Frog & Toad Are Friends*

Lobel, Arnold. *Frog & Toad Together*

Lobel, Arnold. *Frog Went A Courtin'*

Miles, Miska. *Jump Frog Jump*

Selsam, Millicent and Joyce Hunt. *A First Look At Frogs, Toads & Salamanders*

Tyler, Michael. *An Introduction to Frogs*

Reptiles

Aesop's Fables. "The Tortoise and the Hare"

Asch, Frank. *Turtle Tale*

Buckley, Rick and Eric Carle. *The Foolish Tortoise*

Buckley, Rick and Eric Carle. *The Greedy Python*

Darby, Gene. *What Is A Turtle?*

Freshnet, Bernice. *Turtle Pond*

Harris, Susan. *Reptiles*

Harrison, David Lee. *Little Turtle's Big Adventure*

Hoban, Lillian. *Stick in the Mud Turtle*

Hoffman, Mary. *Snake (Animals in the Wild Series)*

Mayer, Mercer. *There's an Alligator under my Bed*

Selsam, Millicent. *Let's Get Turtles*

Selsam, Millicent and Joyce Hunt. *A First Look at Poisonous Snakes*

Selsam, Millicent and Joyce Hunt. *A First Look at Snakes, Lizards, & Other Reptiles*

Shaw, Evelyn. *Alligators*

Steward, Bertie Ann and Gordon E. Burks. *Turtles*

Voight, Virginia E. *Picta, the Painted Turtle*

Waber, Bernard. *Lyle/Lyle Crocodile*

Fish

Hurd, Edith T. *Starfish*

Lionni, Leo. *Fish Is Fish*

Lionni, Leo. *Swimmy*

Selsam, Millicent. *Plenty of Fish*

Selsam, Millicent and Joyce Hunt. *A First Look at Fish*

Selsam, Millicent and Joyce Hunt. *A First Look at Sharks*

Waters, John F. *A Jellyfish Is Not a Fish*

Wise, William. *Monsters of the Deep*

Wylie, Joanne and David. *A Fishy Color Story*

Zim, Herbert S. *Sharks*

Birds

Conklin, Gladys. *If I Were A Bird*

Crook, Beverly Courtney. *Inivte a Bird to Dinner*

Darby, Gene. *What Is a Bird?*

Gans, Roma. *Birds Eat and Eat and Eat*

Garelick, May. *What Makes a Bird a Bird?*

Heller, Ruth. *Chickens Aren't the Only Ones*

Johnson, Sylvia A. *Inside an Egg*

Mizumura, Kazue. *The Emperor Penguins*

Oppenheim, Joanne. *Have You Seen Birds?*

Selsam, Millicent and Joyce Hunt. *A First Look at Birds*

Selsam, Millicent and Joyce Hunt. *A First Look at Owls, Eagles and other Hunters of the Sky*

Shakelford, Nina and Gordon E. Burks. *Bird's Nests*

Yolen, Jane. *Owl Moon*

Mammals

Bancroft, Henrietta and Richard Van Gelder. *Animals in the Winter*

Evans, Katherine. *The Man, the Boy and the Donkey*

Gag, Wanda. *Millions of Cats*

Green, Margaret. *Big Book of Pets*

Gross, Ruth Belov. *A Book about Pandas*

Hazen, Barbara. *Where Do Bears Sleep?*

Heller, Ruth. *Animals Born Alive & Well*

Hoffman, Mary. *Elephant (Animals in the Wild Series)*

Hoffman, Mary. *Gorilla (Animals in the Wild Series)*

Hoffman, Mary. *Monkey (Animals in the Wild Series)*

Hoffman, Mary. *Panda (Animals in the Wild Series)*

Marko, Katherine D. *Whales, Giants of the Sea*

Martin, Bill Jr. *Brown Bear, Brown Bear: What Do You See?*

Pape, Donna Lugge. *A Gerbil for a Friend*

Saunier, Nadine and Marcelle Geneste. *The Panda*

Saunier, Nadine and Marcelle Geneste. *The Rabbit*

Selsam, Millicent and Joyce Hunt. *A First Look at Kangaroos, Koalas, & Other Animals with Pouches*

Selsam, Millicent and Joyce Hunt. *A First Look at Mammals*

Steig, William. *Amos and Boris*

Steig, William. *Sylvester and the Magic Pebble*

Insect and Spider Shapes

Use these shapes for bulletin board borders, stick puppets, and other activities.

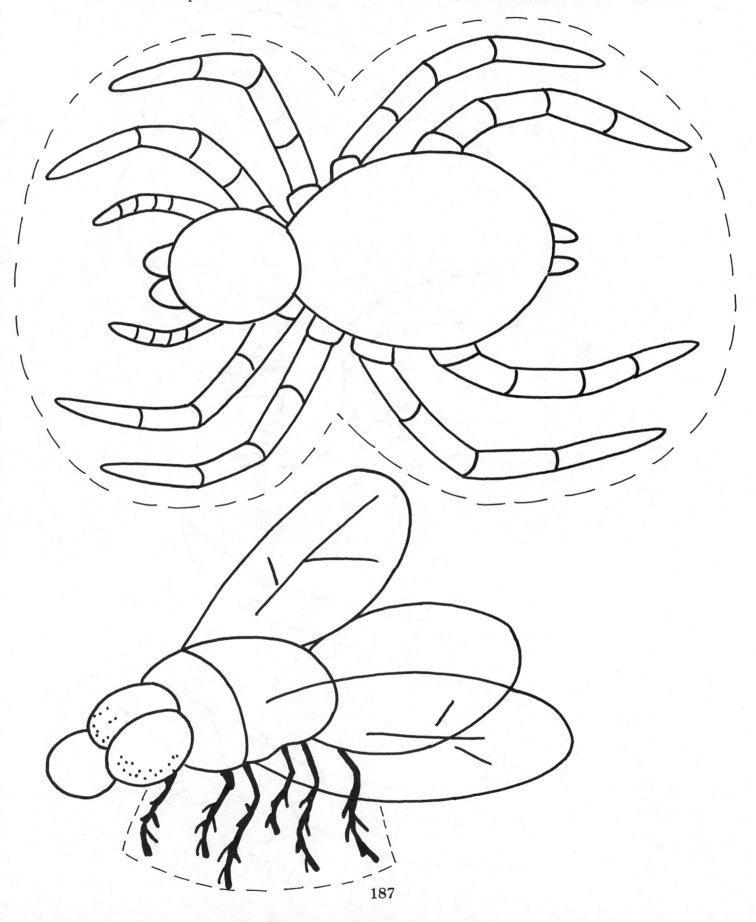

Amphibian Shapes

Use these shapes for bulletin board borders, stick puppets, and other activities.

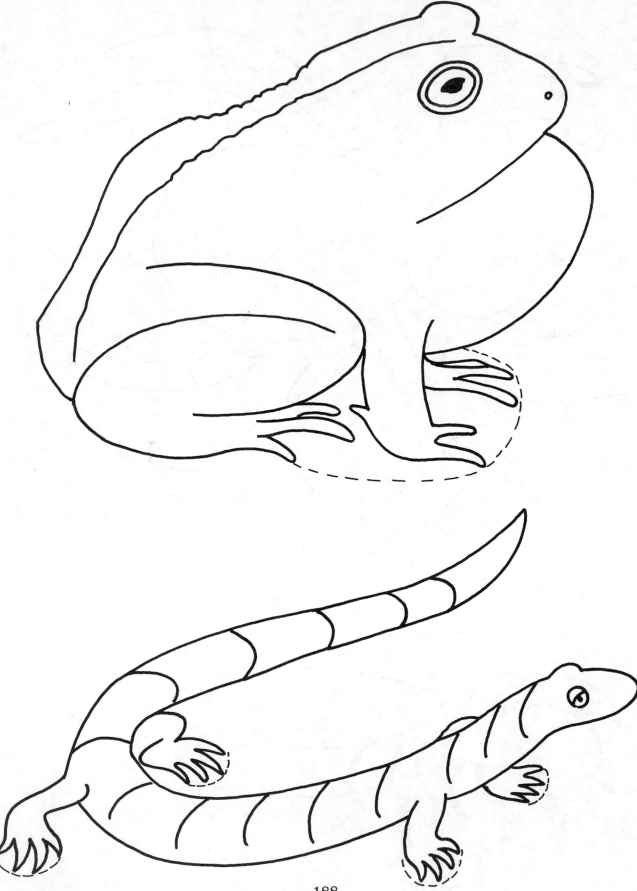

Reptile Shapes

Use these shapes for bulletin board borders, stick puppets, and other activities.

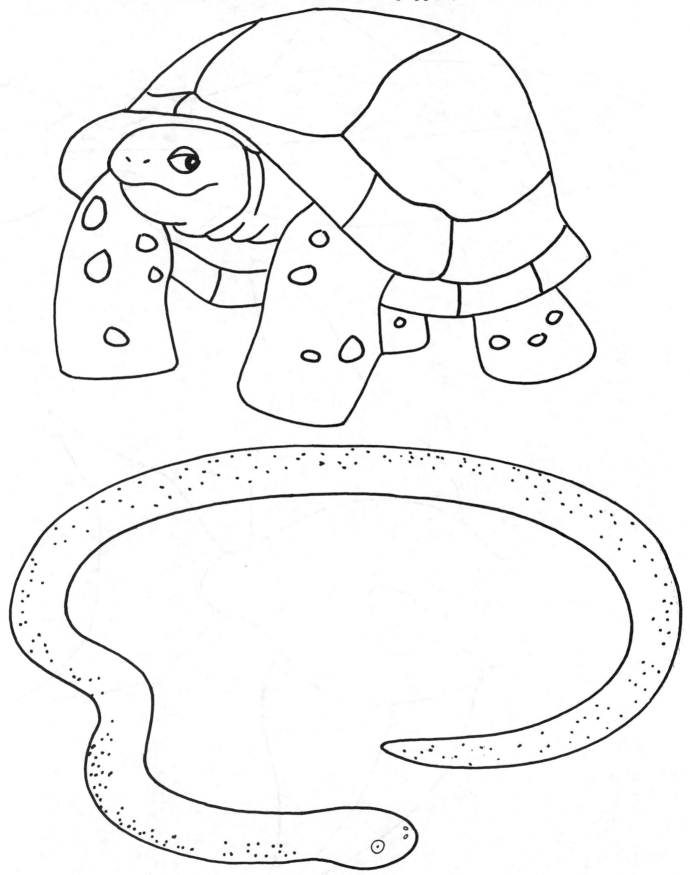

Fish Shapes

Use these shapes for bulletin board borders, stick puppets, and other activities.

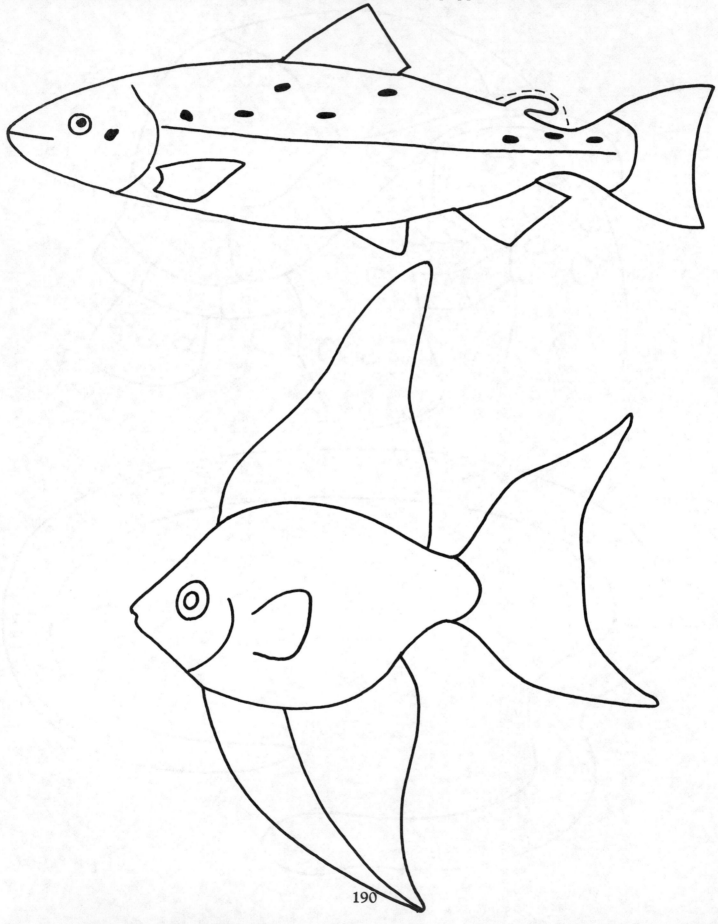

Bird Shapes

Use these shapes for bulletin board borders, stick puppets, and other activities.

191

Mammal Shapes

Use these shapes for bulletin board borders, stick puppets, and other activities.